Table of Contents

Introduction………………………………………………….…...3

Chapter 1: Looking at Yourself……………………………….4

Chapter 2: Law of Attraction………………………………...15

Chapter 3: Setting Your Goals……………………………...32

Chapter 4: Tools to Help You Get What You Want and Make Change……………………………..47

Chapter 5: Improving Your Health…………………....……61

Chapter 6: Improving Your Finance…………………….…76

Chapter 7: Improving Your Relationships………………..92

Conclusion………………………………………………....…107

Introduction

The whole concept that our thoughts can play a role in our lives—that our thoughts can actually become our reality—is an overwhelming notion for most, yet this same notion has been with us since the beginning of time.

It all started with the mystics and alchemists, some Eastern religions among others who started the theory that our thoughts do indeed play a role in our reality.

Philosophers are all in agreement that humans are capable of achieving great things and mediators around the world are also in agreement that when people focus on their thoughts, though meditation or any other means, the world is a safer and greater place to live in.

So if this notion does truly exist, and if what we think does play a role in what becomes, why do we insist on not believing what is and what can be?

This guide is going to be a real eye-opener, you're going to learn about an existing potential we all possess—a potential we have in fact always possessed—but have simply never been aware of, as if buried somewhere in our subconscious.

Thoughts become reality. You really do influence the world you live in—your thoughts actually do create the reality that manifests in your life and this book is going to explain how you can use that power to your advantage.

CHAPTER ONE

Looking At Yourself – Looking Toward the You That Might Be

When was the last time you looked at yourself, really looked, examined, and thought about your life? Where you're going, what you're doing, what you really want? What you're thinking and how it all ties in together.

Most people go through life without giving it much thought. Without realizing that this is exactly the point.

Thought.

Our thoughts are very much a part of us and they're busy creating our reality. Whether we want to "believe" it or not, thoughts actually have mass. They're magnetic, they have a frequency. The good and the bad, all of our minds and all of our thoughts are manifesting around us every day. Your beliefs create your reality. As you think your thoughts, they're sent out into the universe. Furthermore, they attract like things that share the same frequency.

To remember an old adage; "What goes up must come down." Similarly, what goes out into the universe must come back to the place of its origin. If you are the originator of the thought, that is you. The question is; do you even know what your current beliefs are?

Many have heard of the "power of positive thinking" and have frequently scoffed at the concept. To be fair, it's easy to see why so many people have found holes in this concept and have proclaimed it as an enormous failure.

"I've thought positively," people proclaim. "I've focused all my energy and thoughts on what I need and what I want and I've gotten nowhere." But have you really? Or has the effort to focus thoughts and create something positive been done fleetingly, on the fly? The old saying "Life is a journey, not a destination," is probably pretty well known and very true. In order to proceed on any journey, a plan is needed, perhaps a schedule.

In order to begin a journey, a person doesn't simply walk out the door and begin to wander—hoping to eventually reach a specific destination. With airline tickets in hand, a schedule of departures and arrivals known in advance, arrangements made, a person is off on a trip and will arrive at the intended destination on time (or maybe at least close to it). Though the time may vary a bit, at least the traveler can be reasonably sure he or she will arrive at the determined destination.

So it all comes back to the traveler--to you.

If, to this point, you've only tripped, stumbled and wandered through life and wondered why its success on various levels has eluded you, then it's time to find the answers.

In order to become the you that you might be, it's necessary to unlock your full potential for success in life, relationships, and the attraction of wealth, health and more. It's necessary for you to undertake your journey with both eyes wide open, an understanding of who you are and what you want in every area of your life, to have clear and measurable goals and destinations, along with a detailed plan of action to get you there. In order to travel through life one must cultivate unshakable self-confidence and remain on-course, follow the map that he or she has created to the destination, no matter what the inevitable setbacks and detours.

Simply put, there are universal principles and timeless truths that have been written about in philosophy, scripture and science; truths that have been discovered and rediscovered many times throughout the ages. Truths known by such prominent historical figures including Plato, Galileo, Beethoven, Edison, Einstein and other great thinkers, and then put forth by Buddhism, Judaism, Islam and Christianity. Once these truths have been uncovered or revealed, travelers can use them to guide them on their journeys.

And it takes more than happy thoughts about where you want to go to get you there, or sixty seconds of concentrated 'positive thinking' to manifest results.

First, you must get to know yourself. Spend some time with yourself. Consider the you that you want to become, the life you want to live. Perhaps keep a pen and paper nearby as you get to know yourself better. There is much to discover about yourself in order to manifest the positive instead of the negative.

Ask yourself how you're feeling. Emotions tell us a lot about ourselves and others. Because of that, they're valuable tools that give us insight into what we're thinking. If you're feeling bad, what thoughts are you having? It's simply not possible to be feeling wonderful while thinking dark, black and unsettled thoughts.

You are the thinker. Listen to your thoughts and really listen to what you say, what you put out into the universe. You have the chance to change, not your life for the better, but the direction of the planet. The you that you are transmits thoughts at the frequency you determine (positive or negative) out into the universe. With magnetic force, what you put out comes back to you. You are the source. You are the transmitter and the receiver.

It's a bit scary, and exhilarating, to consider the thoughts you're putting out into the universe right now are creating the life you will experience in the future. Does that make you want to change what you're thinking? Does it give you pause to consider what negativity you may be putting out there? The universe doesn't pick up on "don't", "no" and "not". It is much more simple and direct than that. The focus of your thoughts is the focus of the universe. So, when you make statements whether out loud or to yourself, such as "I don't want to fight anymore," that is attracting exactly what the thought vibrates on—which is fighting. In essence, that negative thought is asking the universe to give you more fighting. If you think "I don't want to catch the flu this year," that's exactly what you'll attract. The things you are thinking about are the things you will find in your life.

It's all in your hands. You can change what you're thinking and thus, the frequency on which you are transmitting. Because your thoughts become things, it is within your power to change the direction of your life by changing your thoughts. So, instead of "you don't want," "no," or any negativity, channel your efforts to what you actually do want.

Consider these things when getting to know yourself and pondering the journey you want to take to the you which you will soon become.

What activities in life give you the greatest sense of meaning and purpose? What is it you do that makes you feel good deep down, makes you want to keep on doing it and never quit? What is it that you do, that doing is its own reward and you worry about nothing else at the time?

What do you think about most of the time? Your work? World events? Daydreams about how you'd rather be living your life? People you care about? Money you'd like to have? Do you talk about those things all the time as well?

What do you want? What don't you want? Take a good long look at your life, the way it is right now, and think about how your own thinking has created your world. What are the things you can change?

What is the biggest problem that would translate into the biggest source of negativity in your life right now? Pierce the veil, look inside and determine how you're responsible for the situation.

Once you've taken the time for some self examination and getting to know yourself, you are in the position you need to be to create your life.

Thinking happy thoughts won't get you to where you want to be. In order to get what you want, you must expect the things you want and refrain from expecting the things you don't want.

While you're on this journey of self discovery and orientation, consider that gratitude is a powerful emotion to put out into the universe. It shifts the energy you put out into a powerful magnet that directs more of what you want back into your life. Being grateful for what you already have will attract more good things into your life.

What do you already have to be grateful for? A loving family? A great job? Good health? A little money in the bank? Do you have things as basic as food to eat and a roof over your head? Gratitude is a powerful tool. Give thanks for everything good in your life. And while you're at it, give thanks for what it is you want, what you're working to attract into your life. It delivers a cosmic punch and a stronger boost to what you desire.

And, as you analyze yourself and think about what you want, desire and need, remember as you begin to alter your way of thinking that in order to consciously change the way you create your world through your thoughts it must not become a fleeting one-time event, not an on-the-fly I'll-toss-a-few-thoughts-in-that-direction thing. It must become habitual, a habit you never break.

Another thing you need to consider on your 'you' journey, in getting to know yourself better in order to understand how you create is the more perpetual the thoughts, the more strongly the same thing is channeled into your life.

Do you make excuses all the time as to why things don't go the way you say you want? Think about your excuses. Determine in your own mind that they are in fact

NOT based on anything other than your thoughts and let your actions follow.

Stop blaming other people for anything in your life and accept complete responsibility for every aspect of your life.

Just thinking about it won't do it. The new 'you' must believe. And believing is more than thinking about something. It involves action, speech and thought. And such belief must entail living as though what you're asking for is already a part of your life.

You are a powerful, creative being. All people are. Hopefully, through your journey of self discovery, you will seek a new self awareness and self-understanding that realization will simply take root and grow within you.

Sitting quietly? Unless you're meditating (and even sometimes then) thoughts are flowing through your mind. What will I cook for dinner? Got to remember the dentist appointment tomorrow. Will my best friend call? Should I call him or her? Did I balance the checkbook? Have I forgotten something? Why the heck didn't I win the lottery, bills are coming due.

If you're reading a newspaper or a book, you're also thinking—probably forming opinions or being swept into the story. Maybe you discuss what you're reading, talk about it at length, forming new thoughts.

Wise people throughout history have been telling us the same thing: philosophers, scientists, inventors, theologians. You are always creating with your thoughts. You have it within your ability to change everything within your life, to redirect or enhance. Changing the direction of your thoughts will change the direction of your life – for better or worse. The past has nothing to do with what you will create in the future. What has happened in your life has no bearing. By opening your eyes and your mind, everything you want to change will change.

And if you haven't been truly aware of your thoughts to this point, you should now be aware. Even as you read these words, thoughts are forming, moving and being sent out into the universe on the frequency of your determining. The thoughts you think the most dominate and because of that, your life mirrors back those thoughts.

All disciplines are pointing to this reality. When spirituality, science and logic begin to converge from all corners, there can be no doubt as to the validity of this "rediscovery". It's a rediscovery since even the ancients already had a handle on the truth of thoughts becoming reality.

The beauty of it all is people are thinking animals. We have minds that can determine what it is we want and we can unlock our creativity to move forward, creating every day. Creativity is not just painting a beautiful picture, writing a fascinating book or sculpting a statue that is a work of genius. It's more and everyone has the ability to create their own lives.

In a world where quantum physicists tell us we affect something by simply observing it—that something can be at two places at the same time. That cursing at or blessing a glass of water can change its structure so that when frozen, the crystals of one appear beautiful while the other is mangled and disrupted. In such a world, why do we find it difficult to realize that we create with our thoughts? Scientific work is melding with the spiritual and philosophical and, slowly, we are coming to grips with the unfathomable power of the human mind to create.

And, not only do thoughts create our own lives, but they impact powerfully on the creation of the world. Looking at the world today, doesn't it make sense? You and I are the transmitters. You are broadcasting every moment that you think.

So what kind of "you" do you want to be? With all the power in the universe to create at your fingertips right now, because now is when you are thinking, you can change and guide your thinking. You can choose not to think negative thoughts. You can even have a 'do over' by choosing to rub out some previous thoughts that weren't good for you and replace them with good thoughts.

You can take charge, be aware of your thoughts and create the parameters. You can know your life is good and will be even better. You can shed thoughts and beliefs that have hampered you through your life. You can be the master of your thoughts.

Take charge, understand who you are and decide who and what you want to be, what you want to do in this life, what you want to have, what brings you joy. Transmitting it out into the universe on the frequency of the positive will bring it all rebounding back to you, the broadcaster. Envision it, think about it and talk about it. Repeat without self doubt and with the penultimate self confidence what you envision your life will be. Yes, "you can" is a powerful mantra. Bring it into your life. Take charge and remember your potential is unlimited.

Chapter 2
Law of Attraction – Edging Toward the Light

It's imperative to understand, accept and believe that everything coming into your life is being attracted by you. There are many ways this manifests, but the source is the "Law of Attraction" as written about by the greatest teachers and thinkers who've ever lived. Most of us don't know how a television or radio actually works but we know frequency is involved, and in order to hear the radio or see the TV, we must "tune in" to the frequency needed.

We all broadcast our thoughts on a frequency and, essentially, what you focus on is what you attract. So if you focus on the negative, on the bad thing one person did to you, on the upheaval and misery in the world, on the fact that you can afford to buy nothing because you're so broke—then you're attracting more of the same into your life. So many people focus on the negative, on what they don't want rather than focusing on what they do want, without realizing that their focus on that negative is what is bringing just exactly that into their lives—time and time again.

This is why

Imagine that there is a solution to every problem you have, a way to skirt around, to overcome and leave behind every limitation you may have in your life. Imagine that there is no limit to what you can accomplish, or what goal you can achieve.

There is and you can.

How?

Quite simply by waking up to the realization of your true potential; of what your mind is capable of.

Down through the ages, the wise men of every era already knew this simple truth, what many like to call the "greatest secret".

It is the universal law of attraction. What is put out into the universe attracts more of the same and returns to the source. There are few things as simple, as direct and as dependable. Whether someone wants to acknowledge it or not, it is still a law of nature and it has no favorites. It does not apply to only the rich or the powerful. Just as the rain falls on the rich and poor alike, the law of attraction also rains its benefits, and at times, seeming drawbacks, on everyone equally.

Charles F. Haanel (1866-1949), noted American author and businessman who also belonged to the American Scientific League, The Author's League of America, the American Society of Psychical Research and others said,

"The predominant thought or the mental attitude is the magnet, and the law is that like attracts like, consequently, the mental attitude will invariably attract such conditions as correspond to its nature."

He confirmed what many before him had already stated as fact down through the ages, that thoughts are magnetic and have a frequency, a vibration. The law of attraction demonstrates again and again that as a person thinks, those thoughts surge out into the universe. Once out there, their magnetic properties attract any and everything that is *like* on the same frequency. Mr. Haanel believed, before many of the current proponents of the idea, that it was indeed possible to attract more love, money and happiness by simply thinking a certain way. That it was possible for the power of the mind to harness the law of attraction and for everyone to be able to apply the principles to their everyday lives.

What does that mean? Well, basically, when a person thinks a thought it attracts more of the same kind of thoughts to that person. And since thoughts themselves cause reality to come into being, then whatever is being focused on repeatedly will attract more of the same and manifest into reality.

A good example is the negative. Everyone knows someone who constantly complains. Someone who says, "These shoes hurt, I don't want to wear shoes that hurt." Or, "I'm wearing white today; I don't want to spill my coffee all over the front." Or, "I can't be sick; I really don't want to catch the flu this year."

To the unguarded ear, all that may well sound as though that person should be repelling bad things, that he or she is very firm in what is not wanted. But thoughts and their vibrational frequency, their innate nature to attract, simply don't work that way.

Whatever is thought about the most, whatever is constantly to the fore in a person's thoughts is what gets picked up on. In the above case, the focus is on shoes that hurt, spilling coffee and being sick. Looking at those bare bones, think about what would be broadcast out into the universe.

A person focusing his or her thoughts on something puts them in the position of calling for what that is with the unbridled power of the law of attraction. And when that focus is intense, the thoughts flowing out—the magnetic properties of those thoughts—don't focus in on "no," "don't want," or anything else connected to them that is a negative. It returns to the thinker what is being thought about. Therefore, the thinker, in the above example, wears shoes that hurt, spills coffee and gets sick, constantly receiving the opposite of what is wanted—and wondering why this keeps happening.

Many of us have heard the quote, "As above, so below. As within, so without." (The Emerald Tablet, circa 3000BC). It is but another reference to the reality that thoughts create individual lives and have enormous impact upon the world. The ancients knew it. This phrase is also very well known among the Masonic Brotherhood. Could it be that that august group has also known about the ability of the mind to create and attract all these many years?

It is simply amazing that this knowledge can be tracked back literally thousands of years and yet today, few know about it or understand it. It is even rumored that Bill Gates discovered this knowledge and that was what inspired him to drop out of university to pursue his dream of putting a computer on every desktop.

And Dr. Joe Vitale, author of numerous books on the principles of success and abundance tells us, "Thoughts are sending out a magnetic signal that is drawing the parallel back to you." Plainly, Dr. Vitale gets it too. And Dr. Vitale doesn't spring from the rich and powerful. He was, at one time, actually homeless.

Man has been told repeatedly over the ages about the law of attraction and its amazing power. Great thinkers have informed us and taught us through art, writing and speech about this law. Ancient writings and religions have repeatedly pointed the way. Each individual human being, no matter how rich or poor, no matter how prominent or anonymous, is calling reality into being every day. You're the one who broadcasts your thoughts at whatever frequency you determine out into the universe and you create every day.

The ancient Babylonians understood it, quantum physicists are confirming its truth and it's time we, today, really woke up to this reality. If you get a Quantum physicist talking (there are so few, you'll really have to hunt one down for this conversation) he or she will tell you that the entire universe was created—emerged from thought.

And what the physicists are telling us doesn't only apply to those people who know about it and have some understanding, it has always been working and will continue to work, no matter who believes or wants it to do so.

In many ways, people living today are self-sabotaging with everything they think. The "don't want" syndrome has been cultivated for centuries and runs deep. Like an epidemic, it plagues us and keeps the amazing power of our minds stunted, twisted in only one direction. By focusing, thinking and acting almost exclusively on the negative of life, of what isn't wanted, people don't focus on the positive, what IS wanted and the good things in life that surround them. It isn't until you wake up and become truly aware of the power of your own mind, your own thoughts, that you will be able to create your life.

Michael Bernard Beckwith, a world leader and teacher in the New Thought-Ancient Wisdom tradition of spirituality and founder of the Agape International Spiritual Center tells us, "Creation is always happening. Every time an individual has a thought or a prolonged chronic way of thinking, they're in the creation process. Something is going to manifest out of those thoughts."

Isn't it time for everyone to listen to these great teachers from all walks of life, from across the centuries and into our present?

The future is coming and you're creating it with your thoughts. What you decide to focus on the most is what you will manifest in your life. You've heard the saying, "You reap what you sow". That's basic knowledge and it doesn't only apply to agriculture! Thoughts are like seeds and it isn't possible to harvest corn if you've planted watermelon. Like attracts like. Plant corn, harvest corn.

Now here's the rub, or the catch if you like—the law of attraction is constantly at work, whether you or I am aware of it or not. So you may not even be aware of the predominant thoughts you're holding in your consciousness. Your unconscious may be generating thoughts you're barely aware of, or perhaps unaware of altogether. And since the law of attraction simply IS, has no favorites or understanding of its own, you may not have known what thoughts or what frequency you have been projecting out into the universe.

The good news is it doesn't matter what you've thought or done in the past. Now, right this minute, as you're reading this, thinking about the laws of attraction, coming to understanding, you're awakening your consciousness and you'll never be blind to it again. Once awakened to the power you possess through your thoughts, you'll realize your life really is in your own hands. From this point forward, it is within your power to choose your thoughts and create the life you want. And that means every aspect of your life can be changed by your thinking, there is nothing that can't be affected, no situation you face that is hopeless.

Dr. Fred Alan Wolf, Ph.D, physicist, writer and lecturer, well known for his work in theoretical physics and his work in quantum physics and consciousness is, himself, amazed by Quantum physics. He tells us, "Quantum physics says that you can't have a universe without mind entering into it, and that the mind is actually shaping the very thing that is being perceived."

Once more, we're being told now through science that the mind is shaping what is being perceived. And yet again, it comes back to what you are putting out into the universe, what you are broadcasting. You think the thoughts and those thoughts are reflected back to you as the source. Thus, you create your life.

Television sparks thoughts, something you hear on the radio. Driving in the car presents an opportunity for more thought, chatting on the phone as well. It's a noisy world there inside your head. It seems as though the only time we don't think is when we're asleep, but remember, the universe's law of attraction doesn't stop just because we sleep. No, it keeps on working on whatever the last thought or thoughts were as you fell asleep. With that in mind, when you drift off to sleep it is worth making those last conscious thoughts good ones. Something positive about the coming day wouldn't be a bad idea at all.

If all of this seems a bit hard to take in, analyze and understand—remember, the law of attraction is the law of creation. If you get a quantum physicist to talk to you, he or she will explain that the entire universe emerged from thought. Everyone creates their lives through their thoughts and the law of attraction. Everyone. It doesn't matter if you believe it, if you're aware of it or if you understand it.

Take a moment and imagine your financial life perfect in every way. Refrain from thinking about how you "don't" want it to be. Put it in terms of how you want it to be. What would the ideal world be for you in the realm of finances? A good income would flow. All necessary bills would be paid. There would be money left over for unexpected expenses and enjoyment. Anything else you'd care to add? Want to enjoy a windfall? Think with confidence what steps you can take, right now, to make those goals your reality. Then move to take steps to reach your goal. Everything you think, every move you make will place you closer to your goal. Each thing you do will reinforce the thoughts you have broadcast into the universe and it will come back to you. Your mind, which has always been shaping the world around you, will now be at your conscious control as you direct your thoughts and eliminate the negative.

We talk a lot about negative thoughts being generated by your mind and the unintended bad things that can be reflected back to you because of it.

On that score, there is more good news. It takes a whole lot of negative thoughts and chronic negative thinking to reflect back to something negative. If, over a period of time, all you've been thinking about is what you "don't" want and have spent a lot of time complaining about life and listening to others complain and criticize, then those negative pictures will manifest in your life. Don't trap yourself in the zone of actually worrying about having negative thoughts and risk multiplying them back to yourself.

When you think back over your life, remember some of the tough times. When you were going through them you couldn't help thinking about whatever it was, worrying about it, turning it around, examining it from all angles in your mind. And the more you focused on it, the more you thought about it, the more you analyzed it, the worse it seemed.

That was because, according to the law of attraction, the more you focus your thoughts like a laser beam; the more likely you are to attract more of those thoughts back to you. You are unhappy and pretty soon, because of that intense focus, thoughts that are "like" are flowing back to you and you become even unhappier. It seems to you the situation is getting worse and worse and your mood follows suit. At that point, you're broadcasting on a frequency that is wholly negative and that is what you're receiving back in reply.

There is a simple solution. The thinker, the broadcaster, only has to decide to think good thoughts. Steer yourself away from the negative.

Instead of worrying that your car will break down on a long road trip, decide the trip is a wonderful get-away and everything will go smoothly. Actually see yourself in your mind enjoying the drive, the sun shining and every aspect of the road trip going swimmingly.

Look for this in all aspects of your life and turn away from negativity. Couch your thinking in terms of where you want to be, what you want out of life, gratitude for all the good things you're already enjoying. Tell the universe that your good thoughts contain power, expanding exponentially, and if you slip any negative thought out there, it is weak without even the strength of a newborn kitten.

Your mind is active right now, generating thoughts. Because of that, the power to create your life is now active. If you slip and put out thoughts that aren't what you'd like to see in your life then you can change your thinking.

You have the opportunity to have a "do over". You can replace those less than favorable thoughts with good thoughts. And when you do that, you shift your thinking to a new and better frequency.

It should be our goal to always keep in mind that our lives are now a reflection of thoughts that we have thought in the past, the good thoughts and the not so good thoughts. Since the law of attraction is always at work, and you've attracted whatever has been dominant in your mind, examining your life now should give you a pretty good idea of what that has been. It'll probably give you a good idea of how you should change that.

John Assaraf, author, featured teacher in "The Secret", with a passion for brain research and Quantum physics has integrated this knowledge into his life and his business where he is CEO of OneCoach. This is what he says: "Our job as humans is to hold on to the thoughts of what we want, make it absolutely clear in our minds what we want, and from that, we start to invoke one of the greatest laws in the universe, and that's the law of attraction. You become what you think about most but you also attract what you think about most."

Again it's clear and direct. Over and over, it is demonstrated. People who find success in their lives, their businesses and finances, have awakened to this old/new knowledge. Your thoughts become things. Simple. Clear. Impersonal. "It" doesn't define good or bad, right or wrong. "It" simply receives what you are broadcasting on the frequency you've chosen to broadcast on and spins it back to you in the life you are living.

Mr. Assaraf also points out, "What most people don't understand is that a thought has a frequency. We can measure a thought. And so if you're thinking that thought over and over and over again, if you're imagining in your mind having that brand new car, having the money that you need, building that company, finding your soul mate...if you're imagining what that looks like, you are emitting that frequency on a consistent basis."

And since all of this happens whether we want to believe it or not, whether we're aware of it or not, whether we want it to or not, then it seems the wise choice to take charge, to master your mind and become totally aware of your thoughts.

Leonardo da Vinci claimed, "Obstacles cannot crush me. Every obstacle yields to stern resolve. He who is fixed to a star does not change his mind."

Leonardo spoke the truth. The mind is in charge. The mind is creating constantly. Based on what you're thinking, the future will emerge. And it all hinges on the thoughts you broadcast and the frequency you broadcast them at. If you're feeling bad, it's impossible to have good thoughts. At the same time, the feeling of love is the highest frequency a person can send out into the universe.

Remember as kids how we all laughed at the idea of our televisions broadcasting their content out into space endlessly, and because of the time lag, how somewhere out in space aliens would be watching "I Love Lucy" or some such, long after it was forgotten here? Apparently, now there are some dissenting voices. New claims that that same TV broadcast will indeed go out into space—but not endlessly—and that it will someday dissipate.

The same is not true about you. You are *OF* the universe. You are the creator of your life, your future and a powerful influence on the planet. When you broadcast, it isn't as a mechanical devise. The immutable law of attraction is yours to command. By reading this and reaching out to learn even more, you are no longer asleep to the knowledge of the law of attraction. You have the ability to create a you that you are proud of and whose life is one of accomplishment – which you want to have.

How about you? Are you ready to take into your hands the power with which you've already been installed? Are you ready to reach out and capture the most wondrous version of you that already exists? Now is the time. You are the creator. Have a talk with yourself. Decide what you want to have in this life, what you want to do, what things you want to accomplish. The law of attraction is there every day, always receiving and returning those thoughts to the magnetic source—you. So think of all you expect, want and cherish. Transmit on the frequency of the affirmative and divert from the negative to emit the highest frequency thoughts. Believe this to be true and all that you envision for yourself will be transmuted into the life you like.

Like attracts like. What are you going to attract?

However, this does not mean that once we cultivate positive thoughts, they will suffice on their own for us to await positive events taking place in our life. This type of attitude sounds to be nothing but dependency on destiny guiding our future. Also, we cannot blame destiny for every negative event that we encounter, because one reason could be that that we are obsessed with negative thoughts surging out into the universe.

Depending upon the nature of your thought, either positive or negative, the law of attraction brings you to a point where you need to either try to avoid upcoming negative occurrence or take the opportunity to respond properly in order to have certain positive events. Thus, proper human endeavor is crucial in determining bad or good effects of the law of attraction.

Our response given to a particular situation can either lessen severity of whatever negative occurs to us or even enhance fruitfulness of whatever good or positive comes our way. The actions that you take as a part of your response to negative or positive development in your life are the real virtues that will decide your destiny.

Knowing and practicing this law of attraction is only good for the sake of our better vision and improved mental functioning. To remain passive with pure faith and optimism is not going to help you--unless you take actions. The human endeavor is the essence of life and real secret behind the success.

Chapter 3
Setting Your Goals

The existing scenario of the law of attraction emphasizes largely on the mental activity of human with little or no role of human activity in physical world. This means that what is roaming, running, or lying in your mind will itself be capable of constructing the physical or outer world of the human—regardless of human endeavor corresponding to it.

Let me introduce a novelty to the existing law of attraction: human endeavor by its better functioning enriches the law of attraction and plays a great role. The time has arrived when we should look at this phenomenon with a different perspective.

This book neither attempts at degrading the value of human endeavor nor does it present any alternative to it. Rather, this is an honest attempt to enhance its functionality by providing a better approach to achieve more benefits, minimizing the negativity.

Very little in life can be accomplished without first setting goals. It's not likely a person wandering aimlessly will accomplish very much.

So now that you're aware and have awakened to the law of attraction and the fact that what you think and how you think it – the frequency you broadcast your thoughts out into the universe at – can not only affect your life, but actually create it—you are now ready to make some changes. Since thoughts are magnetic and draw like thoughts to them, creating things, you want to get geared up and focused. In order to do that, it's necessary to set some goals and give yourself a few guidelines to help yourself better become aware of what it is you want to accomplish exactly.

There's no doubt that we live in a world where there are certain laws that that we're stuck with or blessed with. It doesn't matter if we want to or if we acknowledge it. For example, when Newton saw the apple fall, there was no chance it was going to go up or sideways instead of down— the law of gravity in action. Additionally, in order to see that apple fall, he either had to drop it himself or wait for it to drop from the tree.

Now, in his case, it's possible he was lounging under an apple tree and the law of gravity simply 'fell in his lap'. But if he was out to accomplish something along the lines of proving the law of gravity, he would have to have had a plan to DO something. He couldn't be squashing apples in a press for cider, collecting rotten ones from beneath a tree for pig feed, or watching his wife bake a pie and hope to learn about the law of gravity.

The same applies to our situation. In order to accomplish our goals we must have a plan of action and set goals that we can and will attain.

First, at the risk of repetition, you must accept that everything in your life is something that you have attracted. Most folks, when they pause to really consider that, immediately want to deny it. It seems to be human nature and it's understandable.

Who wants to believe sliding off a slippery road or falling down the stairs was something they attracted themselves? Or deep debt? Or health problems? But the truth is, that's exactly what happened. Through the law of attraction, the thinker has to be on the frequency of whatever it is that is attracted. It's not that the thinker has to be thinking about that exact thing. Deepak Chopra says, "You and I are essentially infinite choice-makers. In every moment of our existence, we are in that field of all possibilities where we have access to an infinity of choices."

Bob Doyle, facilitator in mastering the law of attraction lets us in on the unvarnished truth stated: "Most of us attract by default. We just think that we don't have any control over it. Our thoughts and feelings are on autopilot, so everything is brought to us by default."

Now, do we want to just let everything happen to us or do we want to be in charge of the situation? Being in charge sounds a whole lot better and to do that, a plan with goals is a necessity. So, how to accomplish that?

For starters, after having examined yourself as you did in the first chapter; you now need to determine what it is you really want.

Once you've done that, it becomes a process

1. Ask.
2. Believe.
3. Endeavor.
4. Receive.

At the first stage, you ask what you want in positive perspective to get good results out of the law of attraction. It will relate to your dreams concerning your wants (what, how, when, where, etc.). Apparently, you will concentrate on what you want and forget about what you do not want. In other words, positive thinking should be born and negative thinking should be diminished.

Once you reach the second stage, you will believe or expect that the universe will show its effects in terms of manifestation of your thinking or what you have asked for. Simultaneously, you need to clear any sort of doubt lying inside your mind regarding your dreams. Make clear that what you dream is what exactly you want.

You've now reached the third stage where you need to activate your endeavor. This endeavor will be of two types. First, your endeavor in terms of your preparedness with commitment. You must formulate your strategy about how you will deal with the situations right from the very first step till the last step. Second, your endeavor in terms of that which you will require when good atmosphere forms or opportunities emerge.

At the fourth and final stage you need to receive what exactly you want out of this atmosphere or opportunities—by applying your visualization that you already have in your mind.

You need to first determine what it is you want to do with your life; determine what you want and also uncover what your major concerns and worries are, so that you will know what may stand in your way.

Goals can become the incredible driving force behind your utilization of the law of attraction. William Moulton Marsden put it bluntly, "Realize what you really want. It stops you from chasing butterflies and puts you to work digging gold."

Good advice.

Brian Tracy, best-selling author and Chairman of Brian Tracy International, a human resource company tells everyone just how important goal-setting is. "All successful people are intensely goal oriented...without goals, you simply drift and flow on the currents of life. With goals, you fly like an arrow, straight and true to your target."

Along the same lines he further says, "People with clear, written goals accomplish far more in a shorter period of time than people without them could ever imagine."

Are you convinced yet of the importance of goals and setting them clearly? Okay, here's how to go about doing it.

In guiding the law of attraction and manifesting what you need and desire in your life, the journey becomes a deeply personal one. This is YOU we're talking about. So, your commitment has to be very personal and crystal clear.

Get ready because this is going to take some initiative, time, paper and pen and self-discipline. It isn't as easy as simply kicking back; thinking about what you want and having it magically materialize in front of you. It will take some work. You are working on the ability to consciously respond to your life and create your deepest desires.

In connection with goal setting, you first have to know what you really desire and write it down. In this case, the person seeking to direct his or her thoughts will have to be very clear and concise. The more detailed the better. It can be more than one goal, just as long as there is clarity in what it (they) is (are).

And it's a good idea to have a timeframe attached to your desire.

So, you would write down what your goal is and by what date you intend to accomplish it.

Here, we run into the clarity issue again. When you're thinking about what you want from life and your goals you can't be vague and broad. You can't simply say I want to be a success. That's much too broad. A success at what? What, in your world, does success mean? Money? Power? Satisfaction? Soul-moving accomplishment? A combination of several of those?

The seeker may have to spend some time in organizing this.

For example, if you're a teacher and you want 'success' it will need a different plan with a different set of goals than if you're a business man who wants 'success'. If your top priority is locating your life partner then your goals will be different from someone who's listing that as one of several goals, but not the first one on the list.

If there are several goals on your list, the next step is to prioritize them. Decide which is the number one goal you wish to accomplish. Write them down in order of importance and be sure to give them your attention; to read them every day and reassert their importance in your life.

Remember, you're broadcasting just like an antenna, putting your creative thoughts out into the universe and expecting to receive something back.

1. Ask.
2. Believe.
3. Endeavor.
4. Receive.

Teach yourself to observe your life even as you are living it. Looking at the world in this manner will allow you to respond to challenges and obstacles as they arise determining the next step in your journey. As you, the transmitter, become more and more adept at this challenge, you will discover a new ease in handling all that is created in your life. You will greatly improve in your ability to be clear about what you want and about the manner in which you have to project to manifest your desire. You will learn to take advantage of 're-dos' when you stray off course and need to correct. It takes a bit of practice to break not only a lifetime of habits - your own – but to go counter to the programming we've all inherited through the generations of wrong thinking.

So take a minute and write down the three most important goals in life right now. Also make note of what your three most pressing problems are right now. You're not too busy and you do have the time to do it.

With goals set it's time to create a plan, steps you intend to take to accomplish your goals.

You've thought about what gives you the greatest feeling of accomplishment, satisfaction and value. What you really love to do. You may have considered what you would wish for if you could have anything you wanted. You've assembled your list of goals. You've been very clear about it all as if you aren't then what you broadcast could be a set of mixed signals floating out into the universe. Mixed signals out, mixed signals reflected back.

Now, here's where it gets good. As a side issue, perhaps you're a bit uncertain as to what goals to put first— what you really want. It may have been a hard decision for you, maybe this is the first time in your life you've emerged from the cloud of simply living day to day to actually ask yourself what inspires you, what brings you joy and what you want. That is another aspect of broadcasting your desires. If you're uncertain, have a choice to make and don't know what to do – just ask. Put the question into the sea of creation and be alert and aware so that you will be ready when the response returns to you.

Jack Canfield, originator of the Chicken Soup For The Soul Series and founder of the Transformational Leadership Council said, "Most of us have never allowed ourselves to want what we truly want, because we can't see how it will manifest."

Well, we don't have to know how it will manifest; we just have to believe it will. We have to believe that whatever we want is already coming into being as it was asked for. Science tells us that this is true, philosophers tell us the same, as does the Bible: "Whatsoever ye shall ask in prayer, believing, ye shall receive." – Matthew 21:22

Thus spurs the need for goals and clarity – and a plan.

What will you do to keep broadcasting firmly along the law of attraction?

Focus on the affirmative of what you're trying to accomplish. Imagine yourself in the place you want to be, everything has been accomplished, what you've asked for has manifested. What would that look like and how did you get there?

A plan is a pretty simple thing. It's basically what are you going to do to get to where you need to be. What are you willing to give to have that happen?

Now, before you go thinking, "Wait, this isn't manifesting, this is work!" Well, yes, it is work. If your goal is for your career to expand, take a new direction and bring in more money, you need to have a course of action to bring that into being. For example, are you going to expand your contacts, invest in new equipment, do a little more leg work, and examine the proficiency with which you work?

If your goal is to find your life partner your plan may include taking classes at a local college, joining friends for more social events, taking some dance classes, whatever makes you feel good to do. Conversely, don't do something that you believe could help, but you really hate. That puts you on the wrong frequency to receive what it is you're asking for.

A plan, steps to follow, helps you to organize your thoughts into clarity, to focus on your goal more sharply and thus feel what it's like to be where you want to be. It's a roadmap of sorts, one that keeps you laser-focused on your goal.

A plan also puts you in the position of valuing your goals. Not simply jotting them down, reading them once or twice and tossing them aside. Always bear in mind that your thoughts become things, and your current thoughts are creating your future life. Again, what you think about the most, whatever is your point of focus, is what will appear in your life.

Goals and a plan to accomplish them create a point of focus. Action enhances that focus even more. And, luckily for us all, when we take action to achieve our goals, when action is inspired because it will help us to reach our goals, it becomes effortless and feels wonderful.

If you find yourself feeling as though your feet are stuck in glue or you're swimming against a current, then you've slipped backward, you are not acting to receive from the universe—your actions are not getting you where you need to go. Have you ever done something, worked on something, and it felt so good that it didn't feel like work at all? It wasn't a struggle or a burden, it was a blast! And suddenly, whatever it was you wanted was there.

These are the things your plan should accomplish. And if it isn't right the first time, change your plan.

Since feeling happy and grateful, and enjoying the emotion of love are powerful tools to get on the higher frequency in utilizing the law of attraction, then the steps you plan to take to accomplish your goal should evoke those feelings in you. Expectation is a powerful attractive force. Doing something to further your goal with the *expectation* that you will receive what you've asked for while eschewing any expectation of things you don't want, draws it to you.

Working all day, plunking down on a couch and watching TV won't project much of anything back to the sitter of value. Moving forward with your plan, actually doing something to further your goal will.

Visualization is a powerful tool to couple with expectation. The process of creating pictures in your mind of where you will be when your goal is accomplished generates energizing thoughts and feelings of having it in the present. Create those pictures with detail, following the plan you've created to reach your goal.

What will you do along the way? Who will you meet? Will new friendships be formed? Put all those pictures in your head. Feel it like it is today and the law of attraction, always working, will mirror that back to you as your reality.

The more you use the power that resides within you, the more you will draw that power to you. When following your plan toward your goals, you put out an incredible amount of positive energy attracting the same back to you. In doing that, the actionable items in your plan become easy and fun. That, in turn, lifts you to a higher frequency lending strength to that which will return to you in your life.

Goals and a plan to attain them also help you train your attention to where you want it to go. It helps return you to the task at hand and, at the same time, broadcast your focused thoughts into the universe. Why is this so vitally important?

Well, here's an example. Have you ever found yourself trying to accomplish something and your attention strays? It could be happening right now. Take a moment and speak out loud every thought that comes into your mind.

You'll be shocked. It could go something like this: you're sitting in your office, working, and the mind goes:

- The dogs are barking
- What are we doing tomorrow?
- Is the party already planned?
- Wonder what the weather is going to be.
- I should have dusted, there's a layer thick as pie crust on my computer
- Wow, time is passing awfully quickly today
- Stapler is still broken, why didn't I get a new one?

- Sick of all those LED lights on all my office equipment
- Editing as I'm writing this, bad choice, keep going back when I need to go forward
- Tell the brain to shut up

We all have a whole lot of background noise going on in our brains all the time. Sometimes we jump into a project without giving it a thought. By that, I mean without setting out goals or planning on how things will be accomplished. From that course usually comes chaos. But when we set goals and plan things out, we usually move forward with clarity even as we institute changes in that very plan.

To get where you're going, set those goals—set them forth with absolute clarity and confidence that they will be attained. Next, create a plan from which to proceed. Do things to further your cause that you really enjoy doing and you will elevate your magnetic thoughts to their highest frequency. The law of attraction means like attracts like. So when you think a thought, you attract similar thoughts to you. Let them be thoughts and reality that manifest from a clear goal and a well-thought-out plan. Everything you broadcast will return to you. A mixed frequency will bring mixed results. Make sure you aren't sending out confused signals.

And, of course, be wise by responding well to every proceeding that ensues. Remember that all plans are meant to be implemented at the right time and at the right place. So taking no action as planned earlier is foolishness.

Chapter 4
Tools to Help You Get What You Want and make Change

People are interesting. Sometimes it's hard for them to get their heads around a concept, no matter how well presented or how simple. They just flounder about making things far more difficult than they really are.

One example of this is trying to direct people to my home. It's located a bit out from town yet the approach is a very simple and direct one. Nonetheless, no matter how plain I try to make it, no matter how explicit the directions are, it nearly never fails that the person who was given the directions becomes very confused and turns around, finally needing to call for directions again. Then, the second time the instructions are passed along, suddenly it all seems so clear and they frequently laugh at their own folly.

Why did it happen this way?

Quite simply because they took very simple directions and made them more complicated than they were. As if it wasn't possible to believe that it was that easy to get from town to my house. There must be some intricate turns or hidden driveways to take into consideration.

Here's another example. Have you ever purchased an item that required assembling—you read through the instructions and thought it much too complicated, then proceeded to have a hard time completing the assembly? Did it go any differently when you stopped, took inventory of the parts then did the assembly methodically, step by step with no shortcuts?

No doubt things went much more smoothly with the assembly when you gave yourself the proper tools to work with.

And what were those tools? Focus, patience, a new perspective, whatever 'hardware' necessary for assembly and perhaps another person to lend a hand. Using tools of pretty much any description can help a task go much more smoothly, specifically the *right* tools for the job.

The job we're facing here is learning how to use the law of attraction. Now that we're familiar with it, having gained an idea as to how it works, we're ready to move ahead and integrate that into our lives.

Only problem is, people tend to make things more complicated than they need to be. And we tend to not pay attention to things we should pay attention to – and conversely, pay attention too closely to things best left unobserved. Since the law of attraction says like attracts like, it doesn't help to pay close and long attention to things we don't want in our lives.

All of this means tools would be a handy thing to have along the way. Tools that would help you make the changes you want to make in your life and help you get what you want. Of course, that means for this endeavor, as for all others, we want the *right* tools at our disposal.

Then the question arises, what are the *right* tools?

Marci Shimoff is the author of *Happy for No Reason* (and numerous other books), an international speaker and transformational leader who also played a starring role in *The Secret*. She's understood and used the law of attraction to guide and build her life for years. Marci says, "...our feelings let us know what we're thinking."

And that is the key. Our thoughts create our reality, so, considering that we have over 60,000 thoughts in a day and plainly, it would be impossible for an individual to monitor and correct all those thoughts, the best beginning tool would be your emotions. Something you already have and experience every day.

How you feel.

Your emotions are a very important gateway to what you think.

Earlier, we said you can't feel good if you're thinking dark thoughts. Exactly. And that is where emotions become a tool anyone can use.

No one goes through 60,000 emotions in a day. So those feelings, those emotions you experience, can become your guidepost as to what's going on in your head. A tool you can use. Becoming aware of what you're feeling, really focusing in and understanding what's affecting you right now, is the quickest way to determine what you're thinking.

You could be unconsciously focusing in on the bad feelings of guilt, anger, resentment or envy right now.

Or you may be the sort who just automatically, as if drawn by grace, turns to the more positive feelings of accomplishment, love, gratitude and joy.

Which set of feelings would track with constructive thoughts that you would want sent out ahead of you to create the life you want to live and to reflect back to you the wonderful things in life you deserve?

Without a doubt the second set of emotions will indicate a more positive mind set and the more desirable thoughts combined with a higher frequency that's being sent out from you, the source, the transmitter will attract what matches, what is 'like'.

If you feel good, you are thinking thoughts that make you feel good. Perhaps you remember a compliment someone gave you, perhaps you're thinking about how much you've accomplished at work today and how good it makes you feel to be 'caught up'. Maybe you're spending some quality time with a loved one and that makes you very happy. The thoughts from these kinds of events are good ones and put you on a frequency to attract more of the same to you. Great, keep on doing that!

If you feel bad, you are thinking thoughts that make you feel bad. Got a really crummy boss and feel like she does nothing but criticize and micromanage your work? Angry at some idiot who cut you off in traffic and ended up thinking about it constantly as you drove the rest of the way to your destination? Maybe you had a fight with your spouse and kept repeating the heated words in your head. Just as the thoughts from more positive experiences affect you with a good outlook and happy attitude, the less desirable thoughts make you feel bad.

So the tool of emotions to identify where your thoughts are going is a very valuable one. One good way to utilize this tool would be to stop periodically and simply ask yourself, "How do I feel? What emotions am I experiencing?" This will allow you to understand what thoughts you're thinking at that moment.

If you're feeling good, that is the state you want to strive to remain in.

If you're feeling bad, you need to make a U-turn in your thoughts. If you don't make that effort to change the direction of your thoughts, to alter the direction you've fixated on, then, in essence, you're requesting the universe to send more your way. When you focus on bad thoughts and find yourself feeling bad, it's as though the universe is trying to warn you you're on the wrong frequency. You're about to create more of what you don't want.

Think of it as a simple feed-back loop.

Albert Einstein said, "There are only two ways to live your life: One is as though nothing is a miracle. The other is as if everything is. I believe in the latter."

To live in a universe with such a basis as ours truly is a miracle. A universe in which what we think manifests as our lives. A universe that even provides a 'safety' in feedback with our emotions so we can be aware of what we're thinking and work to change it.

And from the spiritual side, Maharishi Mahesh Yogi agrees with the Quantum scientists when he tells people, "All that we are is the result of what we have thought. The mind is everything. What we think, we become."

That is spot on with the law of attraction. And it begs us to use the tool of emotions to recognize where we may go wrong and take action to correct our thoughts before they feed back into something as bad as or worse than the bad thoughts we broadcast out into the universe.

When you feel bad in the future, recognize that you are actually blocking the good the universe is prepared to send your way. Take action, use the tool of your emotions to recognize that less than productive bent and change your thoughts. Shift yourself onto a better frequency, reach for the good feelings. And, once you've changed your thoughts, you will feel better. Thus the universe even confirms you're sending on the right frequency with the emotions that are now positive and reinforcing. Shifting your thoughts, moving past whatever negative event that caused them, will restore that 'good feeling' and assure you your thoughts have indeed moved back to the stream of the positive.

Having a bit of trouble accomplishing this? Just sit back, close your eyes and smile like an idiot. Chuckle if you like. Envision some 'feel good' thing you've experienced and draw those feelings back to you. Then focus on those feelings. As Winston Churchill said, "Create your own universe as you go along." Wise man, Winston.

Another great tool at your disposal is visualization.

Ever get a picture in your head of what you'd like to do to someone who's just cut you off in traffic, or maybe a customer at your store who's nothing but a pain? Well, that's the negative side of visualization. It's a very powerful tool. When you are visualizing, you are creating very powerful thoughts. Let's make them ones that will be productive instead of destructive.

As an example, if you envision something back happening to someone else, those thoughts will manifest themselves back on you. You cannot hurt someone else with your thoughts, only yourself.

Ernest Lawrence Rossi, a leader in the field of psychobiology and whose life's work has been devoted to treating the mind-body connection in people's experiences, remarks, "Mind ultimately does modulate the creation and expression of the molecules of life!"

That being the case, as stated by another professional from another discipline, Mr Rossi, who stated visualizing what pleases you changes the direction of your thoughts to the more positive. Visualizing loving and happy events or ideas of the future, broadcasts thought images as thoughts into the universe which mirrors them back to you.

You can enhance your ability to visualize by starting with small steps. If trying to picture yourself where you want to be is difficult, start with something small. Visualize a cup of coffee or maybe an apple. Once you accomplish that and it manifests, you will gain confidence and ability. Keep practicing. Begin to envision the universe as a wonderful place. See that life isn't meant to be a terrible struggle. Life is good. Create that picture for yourself and hold it in your mind.

Visualization generates powerful thoughts and feelings of what you want to have – now. Let visualization power your thoughts and the law of attraction reflect that reality back to you.

Two more powerful tools at your disposal are Expectation and Gratitude. You may wonder how you can expect something and be grateful for it before receiving it.

Expectation is what you're putting out into the universe when you make a request. Expectation, the solid knowledge that you will get what you ask for through your thoughts and the frequency they go out on, draws it to you. When you "expect" your job to go well, eschewing all thoughts to the contrary, it does. When you "expect" a good relationship or good health or a joyous reunion with loved ones—it manifests. So why would it be hard to be grateful?

Gratitude is one of the highest frequencies we, as the source, can emit. And it's so easy to be grateful for all the good things we have in our lives. That's the place to start. Feel gratitude for a loving family, a good job, a good income, free time, the possessions you enjoy, food on your table. The list can be pretty much endless.

Once you're fully familiar with the feeling, once you can feel it deep down, it's easy to transfer to what you expect.

Think about what you need to elevate yourself to the top in your field. Then feel gratitude for the opportunity to acquire that ability or knowledge and for the improvement in your life that will provide.

If your health is perfect at the moment, be grateful for it and determine in your thoughts that is how you will always feel. If your health isn't perfect, feel gratitude for what you do have and then use the tool of visualization to picture yourself enjoying perfect health.

Gratitude for the air we breathe and the breath-taking beauty of the star-studded universe overhead in the night sky should not be difficult. Think about how the good things make you feel and then add gratitude.

Another great tool to expand your understanding of the law of attraction, the bringing thoughts into reality, is a mentor. A mentor is not always easily found or accessible, but if you put the request into the universe and understand what you will manifest in your life, a mentor should appear in time. The trick is in trusting your instincts and accepting the understanding that life is phenomenal. Too often our 'choices' are unconscious ones which means they aren't choices at all, rather allowing things to just 'happen'. A mentor can help guide us on our journey and a mentor can be any one or combination of many things.

A mentor can be a person, face to face with whom you click and who's on the same path and so can offer guidance. A mentor can be someone at a distance, one who writes books or creates CDs or DVDs that give you more insight and understanding of how to accomplish your goals. A mentor can even be simple feed-back from the universe, letting you know when something is going right or wrong. Open your thoughts and heart to it and it will be created in your life.

Giving back for paying forward can be more great tools in your bag of tricks.

When you receive what you've asked for, what better way to express gratitude than to give back, to help another achieve his or her goals? To give aid when someone is ill by bringing food or providing company to help turn their thoughts away from their troubles—to help them create their improved reality? To simply hand someone change for a parking meter when they only have bills—without considering any benefits whatsoever for yourself?

How does that make you feel?

Good, right?

You feel good. That's a sure sign your emotions 'tool' is letting you know you're on the right frequency to bring more of what you give into your life.

Paying forward is more of the same. When you 'pay forward', when you help someone with a task, give food to a food bank, secure in the knowledge that you will always have more, when you allow another to take a parking space closer to the building making you walk a bit further—you're paying forward. The result is your thoughts are on that higher frequency, you're broadcasting your thoughts in love and love is the most powerful force in the universe, operating at the highest frequency. Be conscious of what you feel and what you think when you give back or pay forward.

But the greatest tool at your disposal is the law of attraction energized by human endeavor. The human endeavor remains a great energy source as well as a virtue, and there cannot be any substitute for it. Behind any success or failure, this human endeavor is the major factor, either credited or discredited. Since the dawn of civilization, history has witnessed the power of human endeavor behind massive success or insufficiency of it behind tragic failure as well.

The genius Albert Einstein once asked, "Is this a friendly universe?"

The answer is an unequivocal yes. Having learned all we have throughout the eons, taught by philosophers, great religious leaders and now science itself, there can be no doubt that this is a friendly universe. The law of attraction would have it no other way.

Now we know from every quarter that our lives really are what we make them.

Sir James Hopwood Jeans, English mathematician, physicist and astronomer, made the statement, "Mind no longer appears as an accidental intruder into the realm of matter; we are beginning to suspect that we ought rather to hail it as the creator and governor of the realm of matter."

And Sir Jeans lived from 1877 to 1946, his statement made well before the current revelations of our quantum physicists. He was the first to propose that matter is continuously created throughout the universe. In his work he also said, "The universe begins to look more like a great thought than a great machine."

Chapter 5
Improving Your Health

Health.

Some people think it's something we're all simply born with. A propensity toward *good* health or *bad* health. We're born with the inclination of fat or thin. What we are is what we are and what we have is what we have, end of story.

No, not the end of the story, in fact, it's just the beginning. The magnetic abilities of our thoughts do not stop with 'things'. We can all focus our thoughts on optimal health no matter what is going on outside.

Dr. John Demartini is a Human Behavorial Specialist, educator and author who's dedicated his life to the understanding of universal laws. He got his Bachelors of Science degree from the University of Houston, then studied Chiropractic at the Texas Chiropractic College graduating magna Cum Laude and went on finally to found the Demartini Institute in Houston which is dedicated to exploring and expanding human awareness and potential. Dr. Demartini has known about the law of attraction and the way the universe reflects back on you what you think and expect. He's broken free of wearing braces as a child, overcome dyslexia, and become a great proponent of opening the heart and mind to a new paradigm of life that he is today.

Dr. Demartini advises: "If a person is sick and has an alternative to explore what is in their mind creating it, versus using medicines, if it's an acute situation that could really bring death to them, then obviously the medicine is the wise thing to do, while they explore what the mind is about. So you don't want to negate medicine. Every form of healing has its place."

So, plainly, any thinking person is going to wisely choose to combine the benefits of what his or her doctor recommends and the power of what your mind can truly do. The magnetic, attractive power of your thoughts.

Think about it. Have you ever experienced the 'placebo effect'? Known anyone who was terribly ill, or just had a problem, then took a pill, like a sugar pill, or did something that should have had no true effect on the body, yet that person suddenly simply just got better?

The placebo effect is one area where the power of the mind is center stage. Why would a person get better because someone told them to take a certain pill and it would help them, cure them, but was it, in fact, a sugar pill? Quite simply, when a person truly believes the pill he or she is given is a cure, then what is expected will be received and thus, a cure. It isn't the pill that cures them, it is their belief that they will be cured. The thoughts that they send out into the universe expecting a cure. Immediately, the universe responds by manifesting just that in their lives.

In that instance, all the clarifying, and even some of the focus, was already done for the person.

The Doctor gave him a pill and told him it would do the job. The patient had faith in the Doctor and wanted to believe that pill would cure him in any case. The thoughts he sent out into the universe were clear, focused, and expectant. What that patient got back was exactly as he expected. A cure for his problem.

For most of us, it's difficult to not listen to society's messages about diseases and aging. Negative messages are what drive the commercial health care system and those negative messages are exactly what people do not need to tune into. We would be well advised to mute the TV when the ads for the 'pill of the week' come on and tell you that you probably need it and should see your doctor to discuss it soon. If you don't, what terrible thing may ensue?

Focusing on illness, the possibility of it, the little ache or pain that might be indicative of something major are all thoughts that will draw more of the same to you.

That's not to say you should not have a check-up or see a physician when there is the need. As Dr. Demartini pointed out earlier, every form of healing has its place and it's wise to utilize the help we have at hand while exploring what the mind can really do. Just because the law of attraction exists doesn't mean every individual has learned how to properly use and channel its power.

So begin now, think about optimum health. And while thinking about optimum health, think about what Dr. John Hagelin, Quantum Physicist, author of many scientific papers and Director of the Institute of Science at Maharisi University of Management said: "Our body really is the product of our thoughts. We're beginning to understand in medical science the degree to which the nature of thoughts and emotions actually determines the physical substance and structure and function of our bodies."

That takes a bit of considering and some getting used to. And it comes from a Quantum Physicist. What you think, the attitude you have toward your life, is creating the very body you reside in. To focus your thoughts on perfect health then is to begin creating what you want your body to be. We can all do it and we can do it anytime and anywhere.

Take a few minutes from your lunch break to visualize yourself in perfect health, enjoying doing what you love. Last thing when you go to sleep, believe you are strong and healthy. Don't participate in lengthy discussions with co-workers about their constant and chronic illnesses. Perhaps add a positive comment, then change the subject and give some thought to seeing those people in the best of health.

When you think about disease, give it attention, observe it, and you will generate more of it. Listening to others go on at length only adds energy to their problem. And, if you're feeling a bit under the weather, don't talk about it yourself, think about it endlessly and thereby keeping other, more positive and energizing thoughts from your mind.

Instead, focus on your own good health, how you feel when whatever it is that is currently bothering you isn't.

If it is more than minor, take action as you would do in any endeavor you begin and expect a good outcome for. See a doctor, explain the situation, get what you need from him or her, then direct your thoughts away from the negative – the problem itself – and back to yourself at perfect health.

Really feel what it means to you to be in good health, to draw breath deeply into your lungs, to revel in the sunshine, every part of you feeling glorious. Expect that feeling to be your normal state.

We've all heard the old saying, "Laughter is the best medicine." Wherever you heard it, whoever told it to you was right. Laughter attracts joy. It releases negativity and all of that leads to miraculous cures.

It even helps to prevent illness. Just recently, cardiologists at the University of Maryland Medical Center in Baltimore did a study on just that.

The results of that study?

Laughter may help prevent heart disease. Apparently, we need a sense of humor to get through this life. When they compared people with heart disease to people without it, it seems the ones with heart disease were 50 percent less likely to laugh in a variety of situations as compared to the other folks the same age but without heart disease. What an amazing study. What amazing results.

By laughing, those people are broadcasting at a higher frequency. They don't have room for dark or negative thoughts when laughing and thus are encouraging creative thoughts aimed at the health of their bodies.

What is it we're told is one of the major causes of illness these days? Stress. And stress originates out of negative thinking. One small negative thought cast out to be reflected back to you can cause serious ramifications.

At the same time, one small positive thought can change that. One thought, then another. Affirmative, constructive thought, focusing always on what you want and rather than what you don't want.

Buddah tells us, "All that we are is a result of what we have thought."

That applies to your health as much as it does to any other aspect of your life. If you've had chronic health problems you may well ask yourself, "What other problem is there? What am I doing that I've been unaware of to reinforce this situation?" Work to uncover what the basis for the problem is. Many times, once you discover it, you understand right away where the beginning point of the illness is and can then turn your thoughts to correcting the matter.

Once you discover the core you can work on the illness itself. If this has been a chronic situation, drawn out over many years, it is understandable that it has been held in the body by continual thought and observation of the illness. The worse it gets, the more you focus on it, and through the law of attraction, attract more of the same.

It's time to redirect your thoughts. Have faith in your doctor. If the illness involves pain, use your medication to help eliminate that pain and allow you to focus more clearly.

You can then bring your thoughts to your own perfect health. To how you feel when you're in perfect health, the things you do and enjoy. Believe that perfect health you envision.

Anyone can do this and use it to work harmoniously with the medical attention being received. Opening oneself to the wonder and abundance of the universe by expecting all the good things it offers and turning away from the negative thoughts that cut you off will result in a drop of those little aches and pains that plague you and you will cease believing every day is painful to get through.

Cultivate confident, upbeat thinking and no matter what may have transpired in the past, you will change it. Set goals, develop a plan and resolve to accomplish something each day – whether large or small.

Eliminate stress from your life. Change your thinking about the everyday things that bother you. Recognize them for what they are and set them aside. Don't continually run a tape over and over in your mind about office disputes, traffic mishaps or the bad chili you had for lunch. Set it aside and understand with joy, humor and conviction coupled with any medical assistance you may need to help you through—you really can heal yourself.

There are many instances of people actually using laughter to help in their recovery. Watching funny movies, listening to CDs, enjoying the happy memories with friends and just laughing and laughing. Laughter sheds negativity and with it, a person will release disease.

Bob Proctor thoroughly understands and has successfully applied the Law of Attraction to his life. His metamorphosis from an early life with no formal education and no business connections or experience, into the self-made multi-millionaire who globe hops to teach people how to re-program themselves for success in everything they undertake makes the simple statement, "Disease cannot live in a body that's in a healthy emotional state. Your body is casting off millions of cells every second, and it's also creating millions of cells at the same time."

Everyone pretty much knows that. But what Bob Proctor understands that many of us haven't quite wrapped our minds around yet is it is our thinking that impacts us dramatically, creates every aspect of our lives. Cells are being created every second of the day. Parts of our bodies are regenerating at different rates, moving us along, and the thoughts we think, the affirmative or negative thoughts being broadcast by our minds, determine what we become.

Science has proven each person's entire body is brand new every few years. Holding that thought as reality then, how can illness remain in a body over a period of many years?

Quite simply, think constantly about a disease, hold it close, talk about it frequently and you can have it with you for a lifetime. Cast off those negative impressions, picture yourself in perfect health and feel it deep within and that paradigm will shift.

Our weight is another state people seem to believe they're trapped in. So many say, "I can't help it, I just can't lose weight. I'm fat and I always will be."

Well, there's a recipe for just that. That belief is stuck in a person's mind. Something repeated endlessly and supported by low self-esteem. It doesn't have to be that way; the negative thoughts can be banished.

Weight is an issue to be sorted out like any other.

First, if you've decided you need to lose some weight, think of it in terms of what you'll look like and feel like at your perfect weight. What clothes you'll wear, what events you might attend looking the way you expect to look when those extra pounds are gone. Avoid thoughts like, "I have to lose 20 pounds by the holidays!" Instead, focus like a laser on that weight you feel is perfect for you.

While focused on that thought, feel the feelings being that perfect weight will give you. Avoid feeling bad about yourself. That course does nothing for you and only blocks the love and, by extension, you will attract even more situations and people who will continue to make you feel bad about yourself. Focus instead on the law of attraction and what you're attracting to you.

And, of course, have a goal. Hold your perfect weight in your head. Be thankful for the weight you've lost even before it happens. And, do things that move you toward that perfect weight. Park well away from the building when going shopping and walk that extra distance briskly with the image of how you're going to look in those fabulous new jeans and new body fixed in your mind.

Think affirmatively, every time your body moves, in effect exercises, about how it benefits your body creating the new healthier, svelte you. Veer away from eating things that you feel badly about eating.

If you are angry at yourself or feel you've somehow failed by eating a particular thing, don't eat it. Don't allow that to enter your thought pattern with negativity that will work against the affirmative thinking you're creating.

Create that image of where you expect to be in your mind and keep your thoughts focused on it. Do things that support that thinking and again, focus on those things that make you feel good and allow you to hold that visualization of your perfect you in your mind.

Aging falls into the same category. Our society has deeply ingrained in us that when we get older we'll suffer aches and pains, our vision may not be what it used to be and the body is breaking down.

Don't listen to it and don't believe it. Don't allow your thoughts to settle on what you've been told and seen demonstrated so often.

Put your focus instead on perfect heath and eternal youth. Visualize yourself as you were when you were a kid, as flexible and happy with perfect eyesight and no nagging aches and pains. If you played a sport, visualize yourself as playing at your peak. Feel the rush of accomplishment when you played and really felt good about what you'd done. Believe you have that body and feel the excitement and gratitude for feeling so good, so vibrant and alive.

It's important to bear in mind that time and size are things that don't exist in the universe. The idea of time passing, carrying you to an older age that is in your thoughts does not exist. You are creating it with your thoughts. The power lies within you to bring about whatever you desire.

Our society has become fixated on age; it seems at times it's all we can think about. Demographics, sales figures, which age block is buying what product, which age group is having the most health problems. Turn your thoughts away from that negativity and focus instead on perfect health. Understand that beliefs about aging are all in your mind and frequently put there by someone else, then believed and held there by you.

Your thoughts and your life are in your hands. You can think your way to perfect health, your perfect weight, and living a youthful life all your life. By thinking constant thoughts of perfection, of the way you see yourself and the way you see yourself living your life, you create what your life is and what it will be.

Remember, your body's natural state is one of wellness. Illness is something you 'catch' when you've summoned it to you, not intentionally, but through some unthinking thought and supporting action. If you've found yourself in a state of illness, don't talk endlessly about it. Find ways to laugh and turn your thoughts to more productive things. Decide your eyesight is good, your hearing is good and your body is great, serving you magnificently and will continue to do so all through your long and healthy life.

Science tells us too that happier thoughts lead to a happier biochemistry. Negative thoughts, to our minds stress, can seriously damage the body and create problems for the mind. Our thoughts and emotions are what create the brain and body.

But, no matter what has been done in the past, you can change it now. Happiness, gratitude and the visualization of what you really are resonates into the universe and reflects more of the same back to the source.

Being the source your best path is to focus on thinking more positive, constructive and happy thoughts, on *being* happier in your life. Direct your body toward that image of the perfect, healthy, youthful you and your body will do what it's meant to do. It will heal itself and regenerate.

Be happy and positive in the time we find ourselves. A time when we're coming to understand you can change yourself.

You can heal yourself.

Science explains everything in our universe that has a frequency. Your thoughts have a frequency.

Change the frequency and change what you are.

Before wrapping up this chapter, it is imperative to understand that, according to like attracts like, when the universe shows signals of emerging circumstances relating to your health—matching up with your thoughts—you need to take appropriate actions. If you show reluctance in responding to healthfulness, developing as a result of your positive thinking, there is a great chance that you will lose its benefits. Similarly, in regard to the negative thinking with strong association to unhealthiness that is going to happen in your life, you will surely be affected by it unless and until you take effective actions to prevent it.

Chapter 6
Improving Your Finance

All of us think about money, what we have and what we don't at one time or another – or for some of us, most of the time.

If we're among those who believe they have plenty—more seems to gravitate toward us. Perhaps you've even heard the old saying, "The rich get richer and the poor get poorer." Depressing thought, no?

Well, that isn't the way it is, unless a person believes it strongly enough and creates that reality in his or her life. For hundreds of years, even longer, there have been those out there trying to tell people how to live an abundant life. Everyone has a right to an abundant life. Believing that doesn't mean a person is selfish or greedy. It doesn't mean that person has to trample over others to accomplish the goal of their own wealth. In fact, it benefits you even more to lend a helping hand to others as you move forward.

There's nothing wrong with believing you have the right to live in abundance; that you're not stuck in poverty and getting 'poorer' as the old saying claims.

The only reason that saying came into being was people get themselves stuck in a certain mindset and are then unwilling or unable to let it go. For some reason, many people believe all the negative things about wealth mentioned above includes, the greed, selfishness, and willingness to hurt others to achieve it.

All that is untrue and unnecessary.

Over a hundred years ago, Wallace D. Wattles wrote "The Science of Getting Rich." It's a book that's available today, a classic, and it was written by an amazing man. Wallace didn't have much success in his youth, but then he studied the greats, Descartes, Schopenhauser, Hegel and others. Through that study and experimentation he, too, became one of the giants who grasped the principles of the law of attraction using visualization and gratitude.

Using the tenants he developed for himself through his study of philosophies, religions and the science of time, he created, through visualization, the mental picture of what he expected to be. He saw himself as a powerful person, moving forward, an informative and successful writer and he took steps to open those doors. He lived the life he created.

We can do the same.

When focusing on money, so many people have a litany of excuses as to why they don't have the money they need. Their boss is stingy and doesn't pay enough. Things are tough and a good job is unavailable. They've simply been taught all their lives that having money wasn't for them and was somehow a bad thing – that one only got rich by somehow harming others.

With this kind of mind set, it's no wonder they can't get ahead.

Nothing could be farther from the truth than that kind of thinking. And nothing could be more destructive and throw more road blocks to accomplishing a life of plenty and abundance than that kind of thinking.

All of the negative thoughts only create more negative thoughts. As with every other facet of our lives, if that kind of pessimistic thinking is dwelled upon and discussed and reinforced often enough, it will reflect back from the universe as exactly that which is the focused center of thought. The lack of money.

But also, as with other aspects of our lives, it is possible to have a 'do over'. It takes a bit of effort, but isn't that difficult to change the direction of our thoughts. Ask, believe, endeavor and receive – and be grateful. Those are the elements needed to live a fruitful life.

Quite simply, it's not possible to attract money to you if all you focus on is the lack of it. More appropriate is the focus on wealth.

W. Clement Stone proved over a long life (he lived to be 100), by fostering a Positive Mental Attitude a life of plenty was with everyone's grasp. And while building his own fortune Mr. Stone, over his lifetime gave away more than 275 million dollars to various charities and left behind the Stone Foundation with assets of over 80 million dollars that continues to make grants today in the areas of Education, early childhood development and youth development. Does that kind of a life lived sound like a greedy, selfish, unfeeling man who trampled others for his good fortune?

It's been proven time and again by people like Mr. Stone, the more well-known Bill Gates and others that selfishness is not the way to a life of plenty.

It is impossible for you to bring money to yourself when you focus on the fact that you do not have enough of it. In doing that, you are actually thinking thoughts about not having enough. In thinking of those thoughts you are creating the atmosphere, the reflection of exactly that. You don't have enough. You must focus on wealth, abundance and understanding that you always have enough to draw that reality into your life.

Dr. Martin Luther King understood that to make progress, to move forward, thoughts had to be focused away from the harmful and negative and what was not wanted and focused onto the constructive, what was wanted, and look at all he accomplished in his life.

Dr. King was a human being just like the rest of us, nothing particularly special about him except his desire to see change instituted and his ability to grasp how that could be accomplished – and of course, taking action to carry it through.

To bring money into anyone's life takes the same focus, commitment and understanding.

And it can be a tremendous amount of fun. Imagination is a great assistant in this endeavor. Visualization. Play a game with yourself. A game of make-believe. Pretend you already have the money you want and need. Think about what you will do with that money – the bills that are paid off, the things you can provide your family, the charities you can contribute to. Playing games in your head will create a feeling of happiness and feeling happy is the fastest way to attract more money into your life.

Think about how it feels to have abundance, as much, even more than you need. Really let those feelings sink in and feel gratitude for that abundance before it arrives and after.

To accomplish this goal, you might write down how much money you need to live comfortably and leave it somewhere you will look at every day. And when you see it, let yourself feel what it's like to have that money, imagine yourself spending it in positive ways. Really know that it is yours and experience how wonderful that feels.

When you go out into the world and you see things you like, things you would like to have or would make your life much easier and pleasant, don't think in terms of, "can't afford it," or "that's way too low on my list of priorities." That kind of thinking will only reflect more of the same back to you.

Instead, wander through a store and tell yourself, "I can afford that." If you see a commercial for something on TV that you really want, tell yourself you can buy it.

Feel the good feelings that come with that pronouncement to the universe. Feel how much different that feels than those you experience when you actually "need" money. That's because "needing" money is a counter-productive feeling. Your thoughts are then broadcasting on a lower frequency and one that is not beneficial to you. The universe is reflecting back to you your "need". The law of attraction dictates that when mired in that thought process, what you will attract is more "need".

When we really pause to think about it, it becomes plain that dwelling on what we don't want generates exactly more of that. And the more powerful the feeling, the more focused the thought the more you will attract that to you.

In fact, that is the point at which you are actually blocking the abundance you need from reaching you. If you do not have enough it is because you, your thoughts, are blocking that abundance from reaching you. Every negative feeling and thought you experience throws up another roadblock, not because the universe had it in for you, but because it is so very neutral.

The law of attraction is just that a 'law', just as the law of gravity is a 'law.' There is no feeling it for you or against you. It simply is.

However, it is essential to mention that the law of attraction is not as scientific as the law of gravity. But, also, there is no sense in not believing it. In fact, the purpose of writing this book is to relate this law of attraction to human efforts to achieve more than what is normally achieved and to reduce your chances of failure.

It's up to you to create the life you want. To draw in the money to your life that you need.

No doubt you've heard stories or known people, perhaps even yourself, who ran a company or suffered a setback of some kind and fell into that vortex of "needing" money. Things get bad, more money is needed, and things just get worse. It can be a very frightening downward spiral. It can rob you of your concentration and your happiness. And feeling happy is one of the quickest ways to attract more money into your life.

When things around you are swirling into the destructive and the dark, the negative and depressing, that is the time when you must refocus your thoughts onto wealth and abundance and the wonderful feelings you enjoy when you're in that place and the gratitude you feel at being there. Really feel the happiness you have at your center. Understand the universe will provide and it will. Accept that moments of doubt may assail you, but when that happens, turn your thoughts immediately to the more positive, to the wealth that is yours and really believe it.

Those feelings of happiness and joy are yours, always. All you need to do is call for them and they are there. And when you feel them deeply, radiate that feeling back out into the universe to attract even more of the same back to you—the source.

As previously discussed in Chapter Three, set your goals and develop and plan to get there. Leave doors open for your abundance to flow through. Direct your thoughts to the positive building of your life and abundance. Stop believing money can only come to you from one source, such as your job only.

Focus on what the universe can provide. Perhaps you feel you need money for a house repair project and you've been worrying about where to get the money from, focusing on the fact that you don't have it, that you won't get a raise at your job this year. When we say 'ask' as part of the creative force behind the law of attraction, that's exactly what you need to do.

Say it out loud, perhaps write it down, but declare to the universe that you expect to receive the dollar amount you need (and be specific about what amount it is) from an unexpected source within a determined amount of time. You may experience doubts about "How can this actually happen?" but keep your thoughts focused on what you expect from the universe and when doubts appear, return your thoughts to that goal and expectation. Feel the joy of receiving what you need and the gratitude as though you've already received it. Leave the little details as to how it's going to happen to the universe and the power of the law of attraction.

Admittedly, focusing on prosperity and wealth when surrounded by a stack of bills or a failing company is not always easy to accomplish. But you have to find a way that will work for you to focus your thoughts to the positive. To broadcast out into the universe what you expect and the joy you fell in receiving it.

If you're having trouble focusing on prosperity with worry at your back, then set your goals, create a plan and then focus on prosperity. Find a way to remove those negative thoughts from your mind and a way to recognize and deflect new ones when they appear. Do not allow the words, "I can't afford that," to pass your lips or remain in your mind.

Change your thinking. When you go past a car dealership where you spot your favorite car, tell yourself you can afford it. Think about the vacation you and your family have always wanted to take and reinforce, "I can afford that, I have enough for that." Tell yourself that same thing over and over again until your thoughts change and the niggling doubts are shuffled away.

It's imperative to remember that if you focus on what you don't have, you'll bring more of that into your life. If you deeply believe you don't have enough you will never have enough because that's what you're sending out into the universe.

Think about the wealthy people you may have met or seen throughout your life. Those people, whether consciously or unconsciously, are focused on wealth and abundance. They draw wealth to them. You are no different. You have the ability to do the same within you. The universe does not play favorites. "They can do it, but I can't," holds no water. It's a negative thought you need to banish.

Giving money is one way to help bring more of it into your life. Remember how good you feel when you give a gift during the holiday season, or when you helped your son out with buying his first car? Giving money away tells the universe "I am living in abundance." It doesn't matter how much you give, but more the feeling you have when you give it. Giving joyously and feeling good about sharing what you have sends out the vibration of bounty and plenty. Feeling grateful for the ability to share and the wonderful feelings it creates gives your thoughts plenty more strength.

If you're suffering with thoughts of how hard it is to get money, how hard you have to work for it when you give it away, let go of them now.

So many of us have had drilled into us all our lives how hard it is to make a living, how hard we have to work for every dime we have. Replace those thoughts now with thoughts of how easily money comes to you. How frequently it flows to you from all directions. Your brain may try to make you believe otherwise, it may try to tell you you're lying to yourself—but it's wrong.

After so many years of believing what you were taught, that you have to work hard for every nickel, it may take a bit of time to convince yourself otherwise, but you have the ability to do so. Repeat how easily and often money comes to you often. Remain focused on wealth and prosperity to knock down the unhelpful and negative thoughts and it will come.

Now, this does not mean that you should rely upon your positive thoughts as if they are the magic box bestowing you good fortune.

But how, you may ask, can you convince yourself of that when you're terribly in debt and every day brings a new pile of bills to your mailbox? How can you work yourself free of all those negative feelings, of the lurch of your stomach when you hold those bills and think about how much money you owe?

Initially, it may seem difficult, but the trick lies in getting yourself to a joyful place, a place where you can think happy thoughts and expect the best. The creative power of thought is amazing, powerful, and something you can focus on. Don't be discouraged if it takes a bit of practice on your part to accomplish.

Try playing more games of "let's pretend" with yourself. You could try envisioning your bills as checks in the mail, but with a higher amount so that you're 'receiving' more than you're paying out. Actually write down the numbers so you can 'see' the amount of money coming to you.

You can visualize checks in your mailbox in amounts greatly more (try to use specific numbers in your visualization) than the amount of your bills. Use the law of attraction to bring money to you when you truly believe you will receive what you need and are grateful for it. Whatever your method of visualizing and perceiving, you've more than enough and live in abundance—always bear in mind the negative side of the law of attraction.

If you do nothing to alter your course, if you simply groan, allow your stomach to do flip-flops and worry about your lack of money, you WILL continue to attract more of the same to you. If you continue to believe you're 'broke' and can't afford much of anything, then that is where you will remain. Negativity is a very powerful force, and it is not directed at YOU. The universe is not out to get you and it plays no favorites. Do not allow yourself to slide into the thought process of, "I can't do it," or "That can't be me," or "Everything will always be like this."

Realize that we are not stationary. We couldn't be such if we desired it. We continue to move forward. What was is in the past. You are completely capable of replacing those unhelpful and pessimistic thoughts with ones of optimism, positive affirmation, gratitude and joy.

I think we can all agree with Charles F. Haanel when he said, "Every right-thinking person wants not merely to move through life like a sound-producing, perambulating plant, but to develop – to improve…"

So let go of the thoughts that hold you back and block you from living in the abundance you deserve. Find the joy that resides within you. No matter the past and how depressed and negative you've felt, that joy is still there inside you, waiting to be awakened from its slumber by your thoughts. Remember laughter is the best medicine? It applies not only to your quest for good health, but to all aspects of your life.

Laugh and smile. If you have to in the beginning, fake it. Play another game with yourself of let's pretend and believe everything is taken care of (it really is, you know). Believe that that laughter you put out into the universe will return to you multiplied.

Even Ralph Waldo Emerson, American Transcendentalist Poet and Philosopher, understood this concept when he said, "The good news is that the moment you decide that what you know is more important than what you've been taught to believe, you will have shifted gears in your quest for abundance. Success comes from within, not from without." Mr. Emerson also said, "If I have lost confidence in myself, I have the universe against me."

By his remarks, it's plain Ralph understood the law of attraction. When you decide what you know is more important than what you've been taught to believe, you would have shifted gears. By changing your thinking, by coming to really understand and believe that abundance is the result of your way of thinking and the emotions that accompany it you will change your thoughts.

You will come to know that what you were taught for most of your life is not true. You will know that abundance is yours for the taking. That mental power is creative power. That as you turn your thoughts your life will turn too.

And in this opening up to the truth, you will realize that gaining abundance for yourself does not mean taking away from someone else. That is not now the law of attraction works. Have you ever trimmed a plant and seen two branches grow from where the single branch was cut? That is where to focus your thoughts. Abundance without cost to another.

The world within is governed by mind and thought – the world we live in is a reflection of the world within. As you think and believe, you shall create. Turn your thoughts to wealth and abundance. Think of how it feels to be wealthy and let go of the thoughts that have held you back.

Feel good about money. Believe it is meant for you. Say aloud, "I have plenty." Think money is coming your way every day and be grateful for it. Unleash the magnetic power of your thoughts to attract wealth to you.

Again, there is no logic in believing that only your positive thoughts will fetch you the money. Rather, they can only lead you to that direction, depending upon how you react to incoming advantageous atmosphere or opportunities. You have to invariably put your efforts into practice.

Great thinkers throughout the centuries have known this, now you do too.

Chapter 7
Improving Your Relationships

Pretty much every person is desirous of a loving, romantic and fulfilling relationship. And since we are the creators of our universe through thought and the law of attraction, then what we desire will appear in our lives. It's just that straightforward.

Finding and improving the relationships in your life is no different than the concept of drawing money or good health to you. It really is all in your mind.

You say, "Things aren't good in that area of my life. This isn't what I want at all."

Right?

Think about your life and your feelings toward relationships. What kind of thoughts are you thinking about the relationship you already have or the one you would like to attract to you? Do you approach relationships with the baggage of your parents' failed marriage? Do you think thoughts like, "I'm getting too old to find my true mate." Or maybe, "My relationships never work out." Perhaps you don't believe yourself attractive enough or perhaps you haven't ever really defined what it is you want in a relationship.

All of these things and more, matter. To attract a relationship to you, or to improve the one you already have, you have to be sure your thoughts, words, actions and surroundings are in harmony with what you want. Discord means confusion, and confusion means you will be unable to attract what you desire.

Think about your thoughts and their resulting actions and be sure they are a mirror of what you really want. If you're thinking thoughts out into the universe, asking for a partner and a family, are you driving a two-seater sports car, stocking your refrigerator with only beer and cheese and living in an apartment atop a nightclub?

If you want to fix a relationship with someone you care about, with whom things have gone off track, do you continue to do what you've always done? Isn't that the definition of insanity – to do the same thing over and over and expect different results?

The answer here is to take stock of who you are, what you want and then take action that reflects your thoughts and desires. Remember that your thoughts (mental process) should be echoed in your physical activities, the actions that you take.

When working with relationships, it's necessary to consider who's going to be in it – and that doesn't mean the person you're hoping to attract. The first job to consider here is you. What are your habits and beliefs? How do you really feel about yourself? What is your confidence level? Are you filled with doubt, fear and worry? Is what is going on inside yourself aligned with what you are demonstrating on the outside? Do you treat yourself the way you would have others treat you?

There's a lot to think about. And thoughts are what we are all about. The thoughts you're thinking, the energy you're broadcasting either straight as an arrow or chaotic and confused are what is being reflected back to you. Every thought is a cause, every condition an effect.

So, since we're focusing on you, the first question to arise is how you treat yourself. What you think of yourself. Your thoughts are your actions. You must enjoy being with yourself before you can expect others to enjoy your company. To receive love you must ask for it, feel it and feel gratitude for having it in your life.

If you continue to focus on the negative aspects of yourself or dwell on the past and what's happened, you're setting up the scenario to have it happen again and again. What you're doing by focusing on the negative is disseminating into the universe that you aren't good enough to receive love and companionship. You're not worthy. And if you continue on in the same vein, people will continue to enter your life who don't treat you well and who are attuned only to the negativity that you yourself have put out.

On the other hand, if you focus your thoughts on the qualities about yourself that you are proud of, that you love in yourself, those thoughts will send out the vibrations that will reflect back to you and reveal to you more great things about yourself. The law of attraction knows no bounds.

Simply treating yourself with love and respect will attract other people around you who show you love and respect. The goal is to fill yourself with your own positive opinion and thoughts. It's not up to someone else to do it for you. In fact, someone else can't do it for you. That someone else can't know who you are inside and what you are thinking.

When you succeed in sorting out what it is you want from a relationship and who you are, you will be broadcasting that into the universe and because of the magnetic aspect of your thoughts and the law of attraction, the same will be reflected back to you. You must fill yourself with love and the expectation of more.

The most powerful forces of man are his invisible forces – his thoughts. Each of us can use that power to create our lives. There is no catch or fine print. Changing the way you think about relationships and yourself will change your life.

Many of us are brought up with the strong idea of self sacrifice – that it is noble to give up something or everything of what we want and need to allow someone else to have their desires. We're taught to put others first and ourselves last.

But that is not the way it works. If you put yourself last, if you don't attend to what you desire in life, you broadcast the idea that you are unworthy and much less deserving than anyone else. Those kinds of thoughts only bring even more our way. It is necessary to put your needs and desires first, to fill yourself in order to give to others.

Some may scream that that is selfish and a bad thing, but it is neither. Many will say you're only looking out for number one, but if you don't fill yourself with love and find your own joy in life you will have nothing to give others. When you discover what it is you really want and attend to that, you will be joyful and that frequency is what you will broadcast. Putting that joy and love out in thought and deed will draw even more back to you. You will be a joy to yourself and for other people to be around.

By substituting thoughts of power, joy, love and harmony for those of despair, lack, failure and discord, the new way of thinking takes root within you and you change. You physically and emotionally change and begin to see things in a new light. When you are broadcasting on the frequency of joy, hope, and confidence with vital energy you see opportunities you've previously overlooked more clearly. People who will help you accomplish your goals are drawn to you. People who resonate with your joy are also drawn to you. Nonetheless, when there is joy, hope, and confidence, they cannot just be pure mental states of your mind. They will be a part of your real outer life.

In the case of relationships, friends may suddenly be introducing you to new people. You may attend an event and meet someone there seemingly out of the blue. All this because you tended to your own joy first, found what you need and took steps to accomplish that end.

And in your own joy, you overflow and don't even have to think about giving to others because it just comes naturally.

The person you have to love first is yourself. You have to love the way you look, the way you move, the way you think and everything about you. The world outside of you is a reflection of the world you have created inside.

Doubt it?

Take a look around at your life outside, what's going on around you, then examine what you've got going on inside. The parallels will be readily apparent if you look with honesty.

It's now clear that in order to love others, to draw love to you, you must love yourself first. If you don't, you feel bad about yourself and when you feel bad about yourself you are incapable of attracting good.

This applies to all aspects of your life, not just your quest for a good, loving and nurturing relationship. When you feel bad about yourself you feel like the life is being sucked out of you. Everything then is wrong. Health, wealth and love. Nothing will be turning on the right frequency—you'll be attracting only the negative.

Thought is energy. Active thought is active energy. To draw what you seek to you, you must change your focus. No more thinking about how awful your mother and father's relationship was, how destructive and painful, and how you want to avoid that in a relationship of your own. No more reviewing your own past relationships and repeatedly replaying the tape in your head about what went wrong.

Turn your focus instead onto what was right in your parents' relationship. What was good, the times that were happy, then let it go. Think about the good things that worked in your previous relationships, the good times you shared instead of the bad, and let that go.

Think about what is wonderful in you, what is positive about you. Spend some time every day considering your good aspects and what you put out into the world. Keep your focus on even one positive thought and it will be reflected back to you with more like thoughts and more energy of the same kind.

If you're already in a relationship and it just doesn't seem to be working, no doubt you have a hard time thinking about anything other than the negatives of the situation. Perhaps your partner is guilty of spending without thought, perhaps he or she has some habits that are truly annoying, perhaps he or she is continually late, perhaps, perhaps, perhaps...

To make things work between you, focus on what you like and appreciate about the other person and turn your thoughts away from any complaints. As always, with the law of attraction, when you focus on the positive, the strengths, you will get more of them. If you remain focused on the negative, the bad things in the relationship, you'll get more of those too.

Many times it's helpful to get a piece of paper and a pen and sit down to create a list of the things you find attractive and positive about the other person. This isn't a pro and con list. This is a list of the *positive*. The good things.

When you direct the mental resources always at your command, you get back what you put out. So focus on the other person's sense of humor, the way he or she supports you when you have a tough decision to make, the way he or she takes care of you when you feel unwell, their generosity of spirit, whatever it is you find to be good and positive about him or her and to be appreciated. Write them down slowly, pay attention to them as you write. Really think about those positive things.

Consider as you make that list what you can do to really bring those traits to the fore. How you can help shape the relationship. Focus on appreciating their strengths and remove your attention from their perceived weaknesses. Think about and believe in that other person's positive characteristics and the negatives will fade away.

It's amazing how when you're in a relationship and some irritation comes your way, the thoughts go immediately negative and fixate on whatever that irritation is.

To work on making your relationship better, turn away from those thoughts, recognize them when they pass through your mind and take advantage of the universe's totally neutral law of attraction to give yourself a 'do over'. When you catch a negative thought in the act, turn it to something positive.

It is a waste of your time and energy to do otherwise. Have you ever noticed how exhausted you are at the end of a day when trapped in an inner world of negative thought? Of critical and negative thinking? When you feel joy and love, and avoid thinking unconstructive things about other people and how they relate to you, you're energized and feel wonderful.

Well known author and mythologist, Joseph Campbell, has told us to "follow our bliss". Mr. Campbell knew well how the law of attraction worked. When we set out to do what we love, to follow our bliss, and that bliss is returned to us many times over. The only one who can bring joy to your life is you. You are able, indeed, incapable of stopping the sharing of that joy when you are filled with it.

And love, that thing we seek in a relationship and that which we so often find elusive, is not elusive after all. Joy is on the frequency of love and love is the highest and most powerful frequency of all.

Love is a feeling deep in your heart. You can't see it by itself, you can't hold it in your hand—you can only feel it in your heart. And when you feel it in your heart, you can see it then, as the love that is reflected back to you, shining in the eyes of your partner, your children, your friends. In their actions and how they treat you.

Your ability to feel love and to emit it like a radio transmitter is unlimited. When you love you are in complete harmony with the universe. Focus on it and you will feel it returned to you many times over.

This same idea is applied to every relationship in your life. Your friends, partner, children, co-workers, even those you come in contact with while doing business and other small aspects of your life. Wherever any sort of relationship can develop. Everything—even down to an antagonistic relationship with your postman. Perhaps a long time back there was some misunderstanding between you, perhaps an error was made and tempers lost. All this time later, you still think ill of the postman. But wait, what about his good traits? What about all the times he brought the mail to you at a predictable time. What about the times he went out of his way to make sure a letter, perhaps improperly addressed, made it to you anyway.

Correcting an old problem will bring more harmony and joy into your life. Perhaps an apology if it's warranted, even long after the fact. If not that, then turn thoughts to those positive things and release the old negative thoughts. Generating those positive and constructive thoughts will reflect more of the same back at you.

Children misbehaving? You've gotten angry and your thoughts are anything but pleasant. Move forward, not back. Don't let those thoughts churn around and around in your mind for hours, creating more of the same so that the spiral continues on and on. Correct their behavior, then let the thoughts go. Turn them instead to something positive. Remember the picture one of the kids drew just for you in school. Think about that nice warm hug you got when he or she first got up in the morning. Focus on the love you feel for your family and just realize how small those irritating matters are and you put the chaotic thoughts aside in favor of more constructive ones.

Co-workers indulging in petty office politics? Are they continually talking about some other co-worker or workers in a negative light? Don't allow yourself to be sucked into those kinds of discussions. Don't dwell on the petty and the negative. Even if you, yourself, or especially if you yourself, are the target, change the subject to other topics. Say something positive about the person in question and move away from the dark discussion. It behooves us to remember the law of attraction returns to us what we're most focused upon. If we allow ourselves to remain in such a state, that too will be attracted back to us.

In relationships, as in all aspects of our lives, the more we give the more we will receive in return. Again, visualize peace and prosperity in your home, love and joy among your family. Visualize an industrious, happy environment at your workplace, visualize the kind of relationship you are seeking, hold that thought foremost in your mind and it will materialize in your life.

You, as a thinking being, originate positive thoughts. Positive thoughts are creative and have matter. You have the intellect to act in accordance with the advantageous episode following those thoughts. You can create the things you desire in your life.

It is time we all learned to think for ourselves, to create for ourselves. If you take some time to sit quietly and think about it, much of what every person has 'learned' has been opinions, suggestions and statements from others.

Most of it has simply been accepted by us as 'truth' with little of our own thought or examination of it involved. A lot of it comes from 'society', a lot from our family and 'upbringing.'

So, the law of attraction, not able to discern shat you 'really' want, is returning to you what you are thinking about the most, going where your focus leads.

It doesn't have to continue on like that. Change your way of thinking and change your life. When a thought pops into your head consider whether it really is yours, whether you've taken the time to consider what it means and what it involves. If it isn't truly yours, let it go. Learn to think for yourself, to form your own thoughts in constructive vein that will benefit you and create the good things in your life you seek.

Use this power to find and build the relationships you seek. Focus on what's good about you and those around you. Veer away from the negative. Let it go—it can do you no good.

Make sure your actions reflect what it is you desire. Seeking a mate? Make room for him or her in your life. Let the universe know what you desire, then take action yourself to allow that to come into your life. Consider buying a double bed if you only have a twin, or perhaps a queen if you have a double. Think about your closet, is there room for another to "move in"? Making room inside will reflect on the outside.

Friends? Treat others the way you want to be treated and send the good feelings resulting from that out in positive affirmations and good thoughts about those who are close to you. Turn away from the occasional bad thought, intercept it and replace it with something positive.

Co-workers? Avoid office politics. Have good thoughts about those around you. Even ones who have been an irritation in the past have good points. Focus on those and let the bad slip away.

If we always remember that when we resist or think less than flattering thoughts about another we're powerfully focused at that time with emotion to give it even more kick. And those negative thoughts will return to us with more of the same. Or in this case more of the same will mean a lack of what you actually desire – good, solid, loving relationships.

The most imperative thing to understand is that when you embark on your positive thinking, it does not guarantee a good relationship as a result on its own. What is essential is that you must respond to a favorable situation derived from it with all necessary actions or steps performed correctly.

Conclusion

Over the past several chapters, we've discussed the law of attraction, the magnetic aspects of your thoughts, the materialization of your thoughts and desires into your life and how to utilize this incredible power you possess to improve every aspect of your life.

We've noted that since your thoughts are magnetic and have a frequency, when you think a thought it is sent out into the universe and there, it attracts all like things that occupy the same frequency. Everything that is sent out returns to the source. The source, quite simply, is you.

It is a basic fact that, in general, people have a tendency to pay more attention to what they don't want instead of what they do want. They will acknowledge that they want something, but all too frequently, they place their attention firmly and without wavering, upon the opposite—on what they really don't want.

Unfortunately, what you resist, you attract. It doesn't take much thinking to realize that since your thoughts are magnetic and sent out into the universe to attract like things, then that what you're most focused upon is what you will receive back. By that extension, we must realize that what we're saying "no, no, no," to is exactly what we're going to get by virtue of the fact of all that energy powerfully focused on it with intense emotion.

So, the way to change things is to change the direction of your thoughts, give your energy positive ideals instead of focusing on the negative. Thinking about war, poverty and ignorance will do you no good. Instead think about love, trust, health, education and peace. Remain focused on those things and when you catch your thoughts taking a bit of a dark turn, don't expend even more energy on being angry with yourself for your slip, but instead, pause, try to get clear on why that thought appeared, and turn away from it. Redirect your attention and your thoughts to the good and positive things you expect to see in your life – and the good and positive things you want to see for the world. Peace, cooperation, an end to hunger and health care for everyone.

There are many among us who experiment with the power of our thoughts. Philosophers who contemplate that very thing along with spiritual leaders and scientists who do actual experiments that are already coming to prove many of these ideas have validity.

Masaru Emoto, well known author born in Yokohama, Japan, has believed in the power of our thoughts for years and more recently experimented with water and the results attached to what happens when water is either appreciated and honored or contrarily disparaged and cursed. One way the experiment produces beautifully formed crystals after it is frozen, the other, unattractive badly formed crystals. After all we've learned about the mind and its power, it should come as no surprise that the beautiful crystals are the result of water praised and appreciated and the unattractive crystals were formed when the water that was criticized and maligned.

Everything is energy. Your thoughts are energy, and the universe emerges from thought. The more you use the power within you the more power you will attract. Life is expressive and by expressing what it is we desire, we draw it to us. The more clearly we express what it is we want and desire, the more thought we put behind it, and the more chance those things will come to us.

The power you possess is in your thoughts. Thus it is imperative that you remain aware of what it is you're thinking, how it is you're feeling. You must become an observer as well as a liver of your life. Everything in your life is summoned to you by persistence of thought. Whether conscious or subconscious, good or bad, the thought creates reality.

It is not so very difficult to think in the positive instead of the negative. Instead of being an anti-war activist and thus adding power to that emotion and the state of war, become instead a pro-peace activist. If you're against a certain politician, work to support the one running against him or her. Peace instead of war. Support instead of adversity.

Instead of focusing so strongly on how you don't want any more bills to show up in your mailbox, think instead of abundance, what you've already accomplished—then come up with a plan to pay the bills you have. The more you deny and fight against something, the more you will attract it to you by force of your own thoughts.

If something negative surfaces in your thoughts, think of the positive and change the direction of your thoughts. Don't be against ignorance, be for education. Forget about being against poverty—instead, be for abundance.

Plainly, you're going to notice things you don't want. That's the way life is and that's how our brains operate. But from the instant you take note of what it is you don't want and onwards, you will need to get clear on what you do want and turn your thinking to that goal. If you're a student and you don't want to fail a course, then turn your thoughts to the fact that you want to pass your course with flying colors and a high grade.

Expectation is one of the most dramatic and powerful attractive forces we have. And expectation runs right alongside the law of attraction. There is a powerful, creative force at work when we think thoughts of what we expect. The process is straightforward and simple – the rest is up to you.

Ask the universe for what you want – no focusing on what you don't want. Clearly and succinctly put out the thoughts of what you want. Here's your big chance to get really clear on what it is that you actually do want. And as you work through it and get very clearly set in your mind what it is that you do want in your life – you've already asked.

Believe (expect) the universe will manifest what you've asked for. Initially, this can be one of the most difficult steps to take. Many people think they believe and expect they'll receive what they've asked for, but deep down, there's a niggling little voice denying it. Recognize that little voice within yourself and quiet it. Remind yourself that your thoughts have power and that positive thoughts are even more powerful. Repeat your expectation. Say it aloud. Repeat it like a mantra.

Endeavor (preparedness and efforts) to reach what you dream about or have asked for. Be well-prepared to meet any challenge and manage to react to emerging opportunities in correct manner.

Receive what you've asked for. Be focused on whether or not you are receiving correct things without any diversion from what originally you asked for.

Visualization is one of your great aids in this pursuit. Visualize your goals as they will be when you've accomplished them, every night before going to sleep, but do it like they've already happened. See yourself where you want to be, with everything you need, and believe it to be real – because it is.

When a day hasn't gone exactly the way you would have liked, go back over it like you're watching the dailies of a film in progress. You can change the things you don't like. Replay them in your head and change them to the way you wanted them to go. Make it a habit and your thinking will change. With the change in your thinking, your life will change.

We all have a world within and a world without. The world within is what creates the word without. Your thoughts and emotions create the world in which you live. Make them good thoughts so as to align with the law of attraction and bring the good things into your life.

Again and again we return to the reality that matter is powerless, inert. You are powerful. You can originate thought. Since thoughts are powerful and formative, you create for yourself the things that fill your life.

Dr. John Demartini, mentioned earlier in this book, said, "...when the voice and the vision on the inside become more profound, clear and loud than the opinions on the outside, you've mastered your life."

Plainly, you want to master your life. You want to bring into your life all the good things you can imagine and have previously felt unworthy of.

You can never be unworthy except in your own thoughts. Thinking, "I don't deserve to have so much because so many have so little," is pointless and self-destructive. And those thoughts make no sense in the light of the fact that the universe is infinitely abundant. One does not have to sacrifice so that another will have.

You can't fix the world. Yet in changing your thoughts and the direction of your own life, in bringing joy into your life, you radiate joy out and that, in turn, uplifts the world.

You have the power. People like Galileo, Einstein, Carnegie, Mother Teresa and Beethoven have known it. Theologians, scientists and great thinkers of all walks have known it. Your thoughts are not magical and yet what you think about, you create.

The Law of Attraction obeys natural laws, sets in motion natural forces and manifests your thoughts and actions into reality. The mind is creative and thought is the product of mind. That doesn't mean that through our thoughts we can set the universe and all of creation on its ear. The universe will not change its method of operation to make us happy and suit our every whim.

However, it signals our need to come into harmony with the universe, to join in the natural flow, to learn how that natural flow works and to work with it. It is up to us to do more than dream – we must create through our endeavors.

A great tool to help is that of quieting the mind, or meditation. To learn to become still, to take your attention away from all that is negative, the things you don't want and the highly charged and powerful emotions that accompany that is to learn to direct your thoughts.

Once you've learned to direct them, to visualize with clarity what it is you want in your life you can create what lies just ahead of you with grand sweeps of your mental brush. There is no reason to make it small or contained. There is no limitation placed upon you by anyone other than yourself. The infinite is within your reach. You are not curtailed by cost or any lack for the universe does not work in such terms. Make the image clear and hold it firmly to you, repeating it and embellishing upon it. You can be what you want to be. You can create the world you live in.

You are creating the world you live in. But, without direction, without clarity, without understanding, your creation is all done on autopilot with no destination set. You must see the end before the first step is taken and hold that image in your mind.

Think about it. Talk about it. Realize it as it is and it will manifest in your life as you envision it.

It may seem difficult at first—perhaps at first glance even impossible—but as you work at creating your vision of your life, as you think the thoughts of where you want to be in your life with more clarity, creating the picture in your mind with more and more detail—it will get easier and you will see what you create come into your life.

Nicola Tesla, physicist, electrical engineer and one of the greatest inventors of our times was a man who brought to life amazing realities. Tesla always visualized his inventions before attempting to work them out and create them. He, too, understood the law of attraction. He built up ideas in his imagination down to the last detail, then held them there as a mental picture to be worked upon and constructed and reconstructed in his thoughts. How well he understood the law of attraction and honed his ability to use it to a fine skill.

Tesla said, "I am enabled to rapidly develop and perfect a conception without touching anything. When I have gone so far as to embody the invention, every possible improvement I can think of, and see no fault anywhere, I put into concrete, the product of my brain. Invariably my devise works as I conceived it should; in twenty years there has not been a single exception."

An amazing brain? Yes. But in truth, no more amazing than your own. Tesla visualized; created his inventions in his head, perfected them there, and then finally brought into being the concrete version of his creation. He was able to see the picture of what it was he was creating more and more complete in his mind, to picture the details and as the details unfolded, the ways and means of manifesting it developed. One thing led to another. Thought led to action and action created methods. From there, methods drew in all he needed to complete his creation. The law of attraction in high gear.

That is the process of visualization. What you can do yourself to create what you want in your life. Following Tesla's example and the example of so many wise people before him, you will evolve a kind of faith that is, as Charles Haanel said,

"...the substance of things hoped for, the evidence of things not seen."

In time, you will develop your own power of concentration and that will enable you to block all thoughts except the ones you focus on your final purpose. It isn't magic, it takes work, hard mental work, but it is within your grasp.

Amazingly, throughout history, we have been taught to look outside of ourselves for strength, power, and certainty. It's always somewhere else where we will discover what we need, where we will be able to attain that which we seek. We expect others to create our happiness, we hope others will see and acknowledge our beauty, we figure others will provide what we need.

In truth, it is within ourselves where we have to seek. We are the ones who create our lives and the world we live in. It is within ourselves that we must create the answers. It is not supernatural or strange or anything other than perfectly within the natural realm when you focus your thoughts and manifest what it is you're seeking.

It's necessary for the individual to give attention to his or her internal world. To make it as beautiful, detailed and clear—and what you create and focus your thoughts upon will manifest in the external world.

There is no cause for greed and stinginess as there is more than enough to go around. Since our ability to think is unlimited, our ability to bring into being our thoughts is unlimited as well. Again, this springs from our ability to construct our ideal within our inner world.

If one views things as limited and therefore, he or she, must grab their share before someone else gets it, then their perception is on the outside in, not the inside out. If you take the time to do some research, you will discover that every great thinker who's ever spoken tells humanity that life is to be abundant. It is something you need to *know*, deep inside, without doubt.

Abundance is the normal. Lack is the situation we have created. People live in fear that there isn't enough to go around. That fear creates more of the same. The law of attraction dictates that the thoughts we send out into the universe, the ones we focus on and give energy to, reflect back to us. So, when people live in that fear of not having enough, that becomes their reality, their lives.

Remembering that the law of attraction plays no favorites—tips in no one's direction—then, if thoughts can create greed, fear and lack, they will also create abundance.

The primary lesson, then, of the law of attraction is you must see, feel, think and live in abundance. Roadblocks in the mind must be eliminated with the thoughts of 'not enough'.

The beautiful truth behind all of this is that you're endowed with this amazing ability to create from thought. You are unbounded, unlimited. The only hitch is you cannot create other people's lives for them. You can't formulate their thoughts and you can't force your own thoughts on others. This process, this ability, is wholly up to the individual. You.

You must plant the seed and then allow it to germinate. Think the thoughts that will take us to our destination, focus on them and discuss them. Believe them. And, while that seed is germinating, we don't simply sit around in a corner doing nothing. Action gives power to thoughts. Planning gives framework to action. Endeavoring is the true spirit of life.

While we are working very hard, tending our thoughts, keeping them clear and our belief in them powerful, we must be aware of the new channels that will constantly make themselves known to you, the new doors that will open for you. Keep your mind open and be ready to act when opportunities are presented.

The incredible power of the find, the force that accompanies our thoughts, if focused, fixated on a problem, will surely solve it. Give your mind free rein to do just that and be grateful for the results. You have the ability to tap into unlimited abundance, so decide what it is that you want from life for only you can decide.

While you clarify what you want and focus your thoughts on that goal, be sure to praise, bless and love what you already have in your life. Earlier in this book, we discussed that love has the highest frequency of all. Love is at the root of blessing. Praising is likewise a higher power.

Think of all the good things in your life and give them great praise. When you praise someone or something, you are emitting a wonderful frequency. See how that person you praised lights up? Even if they are not within your hearing or you only gave praise in your mind without voicing it out loud, you will see the change. Turn away from criticism and see the good. Love and praise will come back to you a hundred fold – so will anger and criticism.

This applies even to those who have been your enemies. Praise the good you find in them. Turn away from anger and hateful thoughts. Remain focused on perfecting your inner world so that its abundance, blessings and joy will spill over filling your outer world.

Everything is made up of energy. Everything is made of the exact same thing whether it is a star, your body, a mountain or the ocean. It's all made up of energy. You may believe you are solid. You look solid and when you peer at your sofa or your car, they look solid. But, in reality they're made up of energy. If you have the occasion to put our hand under a powerful microscope what you'll see is a mass of energy vibrating.

In this wonderful era we live in, we are experiencing a coming together of scientific, philosophic and esoteric thought. Quantum physics and science are in agreement with what, say, the bible has taught. In the bible, the Hebrews have used the act of blessing to bring forth health, wealth and happiness. Quantum physics says we can do the same. Great thinkers from eons past have told us the same. More recent thinkers like Nicola Tesla, Joe Vitale, Charles F. Haanel, Masaru Emoto, Leo Kim and so many others have demonstrated the same.

All energy, including you, vibrates at a frequency – and your frequency changes from minute to minute, depending upon how you feel and what you are thinking.

Quantum Mechanics and Quantum Cosmology confirms the Universe emerges from thought and everything around us is thought manifested.

What that means is that every possibility that can exist does. Every creation or invention in history has been drawn from the universal mind.

You function in the universal mind.

All that you want to know is at your fingertips. All that you want to create, you can. Everything you could ever want to need already exists. It merely becomes a matter of reaching out to draw them forth.

You draw them to you through your awareness. By using your imagination to visualize what it is that must be manifested. By focusing on a need, visualizing the fulfillment of that need, you will bring it into being. You don't have to figure out how it will happen, that is already held within the universal mind. Simply hold the final result in your mind to manifest it into being.

The deepest simplicity is that we are all one. One great big energy field. We are all made of the same stuff, have the same ability to create and the same ability to think and direct our thoughts.

A person who lives his or her life blindly; who has no awareness of cause and effect or of what the human thought can accomplish; goes through life believing if things go wrong, then luck is not on their side. If that person is continually broke, then it is somehow someone else's fault. If he or she isn't happy working at a job, then plainly, some other profession would be better, but of course they can't get that.

Their circumstances take on a personalized bent. It's easier to make excuses and blame others than it is to get down to the real cause and effect in their lives. And that is what causes their misery.

But he or she who understands the cause and effect has come to grips with the law of attraction and the real truth of our universe, and can depersonalize the situation and analyze what is happening. It is possible for him or her to work down to facts without "feeling" the "universe is against him". And from there, it's possible to change the direction of one's thinking and reach out for all the abundance the universe has to offer.

Abundance is the natural order of the universe. You only have to look around yourself to see this is true. Everywhere nature creates by the millions, creating and recreating forever. There is abundance in everyone and everything.

We are One. We have all been given free will to choose what we will be and how we will live our lives. When we receive something in our lives it is through the power of the law of attraction and the harmony of the frequency you are emitting and it is delivered to us through other people.

But don't make the mistake of believing that people have given you what you need. Remember the true supply is the invisible field, whatever you chose to call it. The Great Architect, God, The Supreme Mind of the Universe, whatever. What you received you attracted to you. You are a cosmic being, all wisdom, all power, all intelligence. You are the creator of You on this planet. You are spirit and physical.

R. Buckminster-Fuller, Futurist, inventor, author, visionary and originator of the phrase "spaceship earth", said, "Ninety-nine percent of who you are is invisible and untouchable."

Now Quantum physics agrees with Mr. Fuller and we can see the reality of it with use of our own minds. We are energy and what we think will be brought into being. Our invisible thoughts will manifest into reality. That about us which cannot be seen will be brought into reality.

In a more contemporary vein, science has come to support that exact idea. New doors to knowledge are opening every day. When science demonstrates that something can actually be in two places at one time - the mind reels. When we try to grapple with the idea that something is changed by our mere observance and we are both delighted and bewildered. Other dimensions, parallel universes, are becoming ideas of science instead of science fiction.

The law of attraction is absolute and we are all One.

Bibliography

The Secret by Rhonda Byrnes; Atria Books/Beyond Word Publishing, division of Simon & Schuster ©2006

The Ultimate Goals Program Workbook by Brian Tracy; Nightengale Conant

What the Bleep! Do We Know? By Betsy Chasse, Mark Vicente, William Arntz; HCI; April 2007

Flight Plan by Brian Tracy, Berrett-Koehler Publishers; Aug 2009

Goals, the Incredible Driving Force by William Moulton Marsden

Brian Tracy; best-selling author and Chairman of Brian Tracy International, a human resource company.

Healing the Rift, Leo Kim, Cambridge House Press, 2008

Ernest Lawrence Rossi, Psychologist, Author, leader in field of psychobiology.

THE MASTER KEY SYSTEM, BY Charles F. Haanel; first published1916, Psychology Publishing, St. Louis – now in public domain.